THE COMPLETE GUIDE TO THE ENGLISH MASTIFF

Jordan Honeycutt

Publication Data

Jordan Honeycutt
The Complete Guide to English Mastiffs – First edition.
Summary: "Successfully raising a English Mastiff from puppy to old age" – Provided by publisher.
ISBN: 978-1-954288-35-5
[1. English Mastiffs – Non-Fiction] I. Title.

Design by Sorin Rădulescu
First paperback edition, 2021

TABLE OF CONTENTS

CHAPTER 1
Breed History

What Is an English Mastiff?

When you hear the words "English Mastiff," a few words may come to mind, such as giant, fierce, unstoppable, or even monstrous. You may even know the English Mastiff from the iconic movie, *The Sandlot*. This herculean dog is no doubt one of great stature and strength, but it is also a figure of family loyalty and protectiveness.

Though it may be startling to encounter a dog that can easily outweigh an adult man, don't let the English Mastiff's stern appearance fool you. These beautiful giants are typically gentle, though they can be a bit standoffish with

Photo Courtesy
of Jennifer Tapscott

unfamiliar people and animals, and they will fiercely protect those they love. Whether you're a long-time English Mastiff owner or you're simply curious if the breed could be for you, this book will be a wealth of information in your English Mastiff journey.

History of the English Mastiff

The English Mastiff has a long and rich history. It's thought to have originated in Asia, with evidence of the breed dating all the way back to 3000 BC. In fact, prominent figures throughout ancient history, such as Roman poet Grattius Faliscus, Greek historian Strabo, and Julius Caesar, all noted the breed.

The English Mastiff is thought to be descended from another ancient breed known as the Alaunt, introduced to the European region by the Normans, as well as the Pugnaces Britanniae, another extinct breed thought to have been brought to the area by the Phoenicians. These are mere speculations, however, as the exact origin of the Mastiff is largely unknown.

In the earliest recorded history of the breed, English Mastiffs were known as Molossus and were used as war dogs in the area now known as modern-day Assyria. After that, Romans took the dogs to Rome and used them for entertainment purposes and gladiator fights, matching them up against humans, bears, lions, bulls, and tigers.

The English Mastiff, as we know the breed today, came to England to be used as guard dogs and for big-game hunting. They were also used to entertain the upper class in fights in places such as the Westminster Pit in London. They were even utilized in wars as they fought with the British against the French in 1415 in the Battle of Agincourt.

In more recent history, the English Mastiff almost vanished by the end of World War II with an estimated population of only fourteen surviving dogs. Both English and American breeders worked hard to revive the breed, producing an English Mastiff that the AKC calls "more docile and friendly than his ancient forebears, but no less courageous."

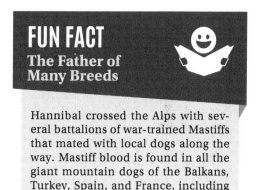

FUN FACT
The Father of Many Breeds

Hannibal crossed the Alps with several battalions of war-trained Mastiffs that mated with local dogs along the way. Mastiff blood is found in all the giant mountain dogs of the Balkans, Turkey, Spain, and France, including the St. Bernard.

Physical Characteristics

> **"**
>
> *The most unique characteristic of the English Mastiff breed is the combination of their size and gentle nature. Their ability to be agile with the amount of bone and thick mass they carry is serene. Their size alone will intimidate a stranger, but they melt when a child is present.*
>
> **AMBER STEVENS**
> *Glacier's Ridge Mastiffs*
>
> **"**

Known as the largest breed in the world and standing between 27 and 30 inches tall, the English Mastiff can easily weigh 200 pounds or more and is massive and muscular in body structure. This breed possesses a strong, sturdy, and square form with a large, boxy head and wrinkled forehead. The dogs' hair is short and comes in three color variations: fawn, apricot, and brindle stripes.

The Mastiff's eyes are set wide apart; the ears are small in proportion to the head; and the muzzle, ears, and nose are dark, typically black in color. According to the AKC, the English Mastiff should have an alert yet kindly expression. Any predatory expression would be considered undesirable in this breed.

Photo Courtesy
of Crystal Reeves

No matter how you look at this breed, the size is apparent in every aspect of the body, from the head to the rear. With a square structure, the chest is large, rounded, and deep, reaching down to the elbows. The tail, which is wide at the base and tapered to the end, has a slight curve but does not curl over the back.

FUN FACT
Ancient Breed

Ancestors of the English Mastiff, the Molosser and Alaunt breeds, have been around for at least 4,500 to 5,000 years. Bas-reliefs from the Babylonian palace of Ashurbanipal show Mastiff-type dogs hunting lions in the desert.

Typical Breed Behavior

> *Loyalty, willingness to please, and gentleness are some of the best characteristics of the Mastiff breed.*
>
> LISA ARMSTRONG
> *Epic Mastiffs*

The English Mastiff is a sight to be seen and a colossal dog breed that demands attention in public. However, despite their intimidating physical appearance, the dogs are known to be fiercely loyal to those they love and are surprisingly gentle in nature.

Though the breed commands a "large and in charge" presence, the English Mastiff is actually very low energy and laid back. Though wary of strangers and protective in nature, the dogs are generally good with people, especially those they are familiar with. If not properly socialized at an early age, however, the English Mastiff can be stand-offish with both unknown people and animals, especially other dogs.

If these dogs sense you are in danger, they will step in and potentially become the fierce protector they believe you need. An English Mastiff will corner an intruder in the home until help comes and will even get between arguments between members of his family. Though tough and protective, the English Mastiff is also sensitive and does not take well to aggressive training or rough punishment.

Photo Courtesy
of Kate Edin

Is a Mastiff Right for You?

> *Mastiffs bond hard with their families. They are not dogs to be kept as outside dogs or to be kept separate from the family. They want and need to be a part of it. They snore, drool, fart, and generally are messy dogs, so if you can't deal with that, steer clear.*
>
> **AMANDA GRIFFIN**
> *Gryphon Mastiffs*

This docile dog is quiet, well-mannered, and easygoing as a mature adult but can be mouthy, clumsy, and difficult to manage as a young puppy. It is important to take size into consideration before investing in this breed, as even a gentle dog is a lot to handle when he is 200 pounds.

Though English Mastiffs are known to be good with children, many people with small children opt to avoid this breed simply because of the massive size and potential for accidental injury.

Size is not the only factor, though. The English Mastiff is also known for excessive drooling, moderate shedding, and general laziness. No matter how large a Mastiff grows, you should be prepared for him to be an inside dog. That said, he will soon be tall enough to counter surf, helping himself to anything left within his reach... which is a lot!

Photo Courtesy of Rachael Parker

All in all, if you are prepared to take in a giant with a heart of gold and a fiercely protective nature, the English Mastiff is the perfect breed for you. When you embark on the journey with your Mastiff pup, you will find your life now full of love, loyalty, and lots of drool.

CHAPTER 2
Choosing Your Mastiff

Buying vs. Adopting

The decision to buy versus adopt a dog is a personal one that takes careful consideration. We are all aware of the great need to adopt shelter dogs or dogs placed in rescue facilities, but oftentimes, these dogs have special needs, medical, social, or both, and require a special kind of home.

If you are willing and capable of caring for an English Mastiff from a Mastiff rescue, that dog will reward you with the same love and companionship as a dog from a breeder. However, you should discuss issues, whether

Photo Courtesy
of Julie Blacklock

behavioral or health, with the rescue before you commit. The last thing the dog needs is to be dropped back off at a shelter when you discover you aren't able to care for him after all. Not all dogs in shelters and rescues have special needs, though. You may find exactly what you're looking for in a pup in a shelter near you.

FUN FACT
Big Litters

English Mastiff moms have an average of 10-12 puppies per litter. However, the largest litter of puppies on record was 24 puppies born to an English Mastiff. 20 of those puppies survived the first week.

Types of Animal Shelters and Rescues

In the United States, there are three different classifications for pet and animal rescues: municipal shelters, no-kill shelters, and nonprofit rescue organizations. Below is a brief description of each.

Municipal Shelters: These shelters take in strays, abandoned animals, and animals surrendered by their owners. They are operated and funded by local governments. The animals there have a limited time to be adopted and are often euthanized due to a lack of space for new intakes.

Adoption fees are typically low at these places. Almost all require an animal to be spayed or neutered before it is adopted. The dogs are housed in kennels and are maintained with basic veterinary care while they remain in the shelter.

If you adopt from a shelter, be aware that the stressful environment can cause a dog to act fearful or aggressive, even if that is not his true personality. This is known as "kennel syndrome." If you find a Mastiff that you believe may be a good fit for you, ask the shelter for a trial period. This allows you to take the dog home for a few days to see if he is a good match outside of the high-stress environment of the shelter.

No-Kill Shelters: These are private organizations that will not kill a healthy and adoptable animal. Because they do not euthanize animals, they have a limited intake policy and end up turning many animals away due to lack of space.

Dogs are often kept in no-kill shelters for an extended time; months and sometimes even years go by before they are adopted. If a facility is full, foster homes are often used. Many times, this can actually help avoid "kennel syndrome" and help a troubled dog adjust and become more adoptable.

*Photo Courtesy
of Anita Halme
Dolph Creek Mastiffs*

Non-Profit Rescue Organizations: These organizations are mostly run and operated by volunteers. They utilize foster houses to save as many animals as possible. They do not euthanize animals.

Typically privately funded or donation dependent, many rescues are breed-specific and dedicated to saving one specific dog type, such as the English Mastiff. Rescues offer the same basic veterinarian care as municipal shelters but often have to pay face-value prices leading to higher adoption fees.

Most rescue groups rely heavily on foster families. Some may not have a physical facility at all but instead maintain a website with information about their available and adoptable dogs. Because the dog lives with a foster family, more is known about the dog's history and personality, making it easier to find the animal a compatible home.

Rescue organizations typically have much stricter adoption guidelines and policies, frequently requiring a home inspection before approval. Much like with a typical breeder, many have policies in place that require adopters to return the dog to the rescue if they can no longer keep the animal. Contact between rescuers and adopters is usually maintained for three to six months to ensure things are going well. The rescue may even require a post-adoption home visit to check in.

Benefits of Adopting and Tips

Most dogs you find in a shelter or rescue are fully mature or close to it. This advanced age gives you the opportunity to fully get to know the personality of the Mastiff before adopting and bringing him home. You'll know ahead of time how the dog reacts to other dogs, strangers, and even how he interacts with children. These are important aspects when you're searching for a Mastiff to seamlessly fit into your life.

If you're planning to adopt, call your local shelters and let them know what you're looking for. Ask them to be on the lookout for an English Mastiff and to give you a call if one comes in.

Rescue dogs often show a special appreciation for a chance at a forever home and a family to call their own. Breed-specific rescues often have applications and screening processes for potential families, so get your information in quickly if you find a dog you love. It's not uncommon to find yourself on a waitlist for a rescue.

Breeder Reputation

Ask to see the contract beforehand and read it carefully. If there's something you don't agree with, don't be shy. Mastiffs from a quality breeder should be sold on non-breeding contracts—these can be lifted when certain health/showing requirements are met. If you are asked to enter into a co-ownership, think about it carefully before agreeing.

AMANDA GRIFFIN
Gryphon Mastiffs

If you choose to buy an English Mastiff from a breeder, there are several things you need to know beforehand. While breeders online may appear to be legitimate and trustworthy, many are not. Because people will pay a pretty penny for a purebred dog, many "backyard breeders" sell their pups for a significant price. The problem with these backyard breeders is that they typically don't have the breed's best interest in mind. They often do not invest in quality breeding stock and forgo many of the genetic tests and screens reputable breeders employ to make sure their dogs are healthy.

At their worst, some backyard breeders are considered puppy mills. These are places that only keep dogs alive to pump out litters and make money. The dogs are often overcrowded and kept in small cages, unable to get out and actually live the life a dog deserves. Avoiding these places is of utmost importance.

Reputable breeders will be established in the English Mastiff community and will undoubtedly be able to connect you with other reputable breeders.

How to Find the Right Breeder

Be sure to ask to see all the health testing. At an absolute minimum, the parents (and hopefully the grandparents) should have:

- *OFA Pennhip testing done on the hips.*
- *OFA done on the elbows*
- *Thyroid testing*
- *Cardiac testing*
- *Cystinuria testing*
- *PRA DNA (either the actual test or clear-through parentage)*
- *CERF (eye examination)*

AMANDA GRIFFIN
Gryphon Mastiffs

A quick internet search will bring up many English Mastiff breeders. The question is, how can you tell the difference between a reputable breeder and one who is not? There are several questions you should ask any breeder when you are searching for the perfect Mastiff puppy.

CAN I VISIT THE BREEDING FACILITY?

A reputable breeder should always welcome a potential adoptee into the facility. Due to health concerns, they might not allow you into certain areas of the facility because there is a concern of tracking in diseases that could

Photo Courtesy of Crystal Reeves

be detrimental to a young puppy's undeveloped immune system. However, a reputable breeder should allow you to come on-site and see other dogs in his or her program.

The following are questions you should consider asking each prospective breeder you speak with:

HOW LONG HAVE YOU BEEN BREEDING ENGLISH MASTIFFS?

Optimally, you will want to seek out a breeder with many years of experience who has produced many proven healthy litters. A quality breeder with adequate experience will know how to breed only the most desirable traits and healthy dogs.

WHAT GENETIC CONDITIONS DO YOU TEST FOR BEFORE BREEDING, AND WHAT CONDITIONS DO YOU SCREEN THE PUPPIES FOR BEFORE SELLING?

All purebred dogs are prone to certain genetic diseases and conditions. These will be discussed in greater detail in chapter 13. Before purchasing, it's highly important to ask for a detailed list of the tests and screens performed on the parents, as well as copies of the test results. These tests should be performed by certified specialists for each potential ailment, such as a board-certified veterinarian cardiologist and an ophthalmologist. Having a dog "checked out" by a vet is not the same as genetic testing.

CAN I SEE VETERINARY RECORDS FOR BOTH PARENTS?

Choosing an English Mastiff is a significant investment that will potentially affect your life for the next ten years. It's very important that the breeder you choose is open and transparent with information regarding the dam and sire. If the breeder is not willing to share medical records, you should find another breeder. Both the dam and the sire should have been checked by specialists and cleared for defects. The breeder should also provide proof of genetic testing.

HELPFUL TIP
Find the Right Breeder

Since English Mastiffs are highly prone to hip dysplasia, you should take the time to find a breeder who health tests their breeding dogs. Find out the rate of hip dysplasia in their lines and what they're doing to reduce its incidence in their breeding program.

WHAT KIND OF GUARANTEE DO YOU PROVIDE FOR YOUR PUPPIES?

A reputable breeder will stipulate health guarantees in a contract before you purchase your pup. Look for specifics in a contract that state they will

Photo Courtesy
of Kate O'Brien

refund most or all of the cost of the puppy in the event any congenital health conditions appear within the first year. Do not buy a dog from a breeder that offers no health guarantee or who offers to replace the puppy with a healthy one with no option to receive a refund. If the breeder produced a genetically unhealthy puppy the first time, chances are they aren't breeding healthy dogs.

Many people are also unwilling to return their dog for a replacement, as they have already become attached. Offering to replace the dog is a low-risk guarantee and should serve as a warning sign. On the other hand, a responsible breeder will always take back a dog that you can no longer care for, no matter the reason.

Many times, a breeder's health guarantee will have stipulations included in the contract. These may include not neutering or spaying until after a year so that the joints are allowed to fully develop, feeding your puppy a proper diet, and regular visits to the vet. As much as a responsible breeder wants his or her puppies to remain in perfect health for their entire life, not all owners care for a dog the same way, and health results will vary based on lifestyle.

Remember, no matter how good the breeding lines are or how thorough the testing is, no breeder can guarantee perfect health for a dog's entire life.

DO YOU EVER SELL TO A BROKER OR PET SHOP?

If the answer is yes, walk away from this breeder immediately. Puppies found in a pet shop are bred for profit alone and come with no health guarantee. A responsible breeder, breeding for the betterment of the dog's health and appearance, will never sell an animal to a broker or a pet store. Reputable breeders are heavily invested in their dogs and will want to meet the families of each of their puppies to be sure they will be properly cared for.

Choosing the Perfect English Mastiff Puppy

Once you have chosen a reputable breeder, you'll need to get on the waiting list for a pup. Hopefully, soon after, you will be ready to pick your puppy out from the litter! While there is a generally common temperament among well-bred English Mastiffs, each puppy will have his or her own personality.

Visit the litter ahead of time if you can so that you can see the puppies and how they interact with each other. Does one seem more aggressive than another? This kind of puppy may be feisty, energetic, and a bit more assertive by nature. Is there one who would rather play alone in the corner with their own toy? This puppy may be a bit more docile and independent. Is there one that is climbing all over you, gnawing on your hands or shoes? This could be a puppy with a curious and adventurous personality.

None of these personalities are "good" or "bad," but some personalities may fit in better with your lifestyle and family. A good breeder should be spending ample time with the pups and should be able to tell you about their personalities before you choose.

Puppy Personality Traits

For a more in-depth look at puppy personality traits, read through the following descriptions to help you better determine what each pup's personality may be. Most puppies fit into one of five categories.

The Dominant Puppy: This puppy could be bossy, pushy, and may sometimes be more vocal than the others. He may appear a bit rebellious and be more challenging to train. These puppies need early and frequent training to ensure good behavior later in life.

The Active Puppy: Active puppies can also be somewhat pushy and bossy and sometimes a little mouthy. While no Mastiff will be overly active as an adult, these puppies may grow up to become more active Mastiffs than their lazier counterparts. They can also get easily distracted, which can make training more of a challenge.

The Affectionate Puppy: These puppies are friendly and eager to please. They learn quickly and are quite easy to train. Outgoing and self-confident, they tend to form extraordinarily strong bonds quickly with their humans. They generally are more likely to get along well with other dogs and animals. Dogs with this personality type are happiest near their companions.

The Calm Puppy: More submissive than others, the calm puppy is typically happy to be a follower. Such puppies can be quite affectionate but need a leader to be in charge. These dogs are eager to please but sometimes need extra motivation during training. They are mostly friendly and get along well with other dogs and animals, but they can be prone to separation anxiety when left alone.

The Fearful Puppy: Highly submissive dogs, these puppies can be quite shy and timid at times and are easily scared or intimidated. They lack self-confidence and can be quite sensitive. These dogs do best when they have a calm and quiet owner who has compassion and patience. Loud noises, punishment, and even light corrections may be too much for these dogs to handle. A reputable breeder should not have any fearful puppies in a healthy litter. If you notice there are fearful puppies, it may be a red flag that something is wrong.

CHAPTER 3

Preparing for Your English Mastiff

Before bringing your English Mastiff puppy home for the first time, it's important that you prepare not only your home but your family and any existing pets, too. While pick-up day may be exciting, there's nothing worse than finally getting your pup home only to realize you weren't quite ready after all.

Preparing Other Pets

If you are bringing your Mastiff puppy into the home as an only pet, the transition should be rather smooth. However, when there are other pets involved, whether they are dogs, cats, or another small indoor pet, things can get more complicated.

Allowing your existing pets to become accustomed to the new pup, even before you bring him home, is key to a successful introduction. Discuss this transition with your breeder and ask if he or she will allow you to pick up a blanket or a toy with the new puppy's scent on it ahead of time. Introduce the blanket or toy to your current dogs and other pets to allow them to become accustomed to the smell of another puppy in the house. Do this up to a week before you bring your Mastiff puppy home.

FUN FACT
World's Largest Dog

The world's largest dog on record was an English Mastiff named Zorba. Zorba stood 37" high at the shoulder and 8 feet 3 inches long from the tip of his nose to the tip of his tail. He weighed a whopping 343 pounds!

When pick-up day finally arrives, make sure you have help with the first introduction. If introducing dogs or a cat, do this in a neutral area so that your existing pets do not feel territorial. Consider letting the dogs meet briefly outside of the house in a less used area but avoid public spaces or parks until the puppy has had all of his vaccinations. Introducing him to these spaces too soon can be detrimental to his health.

The first meeting should be brief and positive. Keep your dogs leashed and allow them to greet your puppy. Make sure you remain in control of your older dogs to ensure the safety of your new pup. After a brief time, separate the dogs and your pup so that nobody becomes too overwhelmed. Depending on how the dogs reacted to each other, allow them to slowly spend more time together until they are comfortable. If any moments become stressful for either party, take a break and try later.

If you are introducing your puppy to a cat, it is important to keep both animals safe by maintaining control of your puppy or by allowing them to meet while one is contained in a crate or separated another barrier. Allow them short, controlled interactions at quiet moments of the day until they are both calm around each other. Always make sure your cat has a safe place to retreat to, preferably off the ground, such as a cat tower.

Be sure to show your other dogs and pets some extra attention and before and after you bring home your English Mastiff puppy. This can help ease jealousy and let them know they know they are still important members of the family.

Photo Courtesy of Holly Rhoddy

Preparing Children and Family

The most important part of preparing your family for a new English Mastiff puppy is teaching them how to properly handle him. If you have small children, it's important to teach them not to hit, tug on ears or tails, or poke eyes. While English Mastiff puppies aren't small or delicate, children should still learn to be respectful so that positive relationships can form. Careful supervision should always be maintained with small children and puppies, even if you think the situation is safe.

Aside from teaching children how to properly handle a puppy, make sure the whole family is on board and has realistic expectations for how life will change with a new pup. It may even be beneficial to go over responsibilities and determine who will do what before bringing your Mastiff home.

How to Puppy Proof Your Home

66

It's always a good idea to puppy-proof your home as you would if you were bringing home a new baby. Make sure all breakables are out of reach and there are plenty of safe toys to distract the new puppy from getting into things he shouldn't.

MELISSA COX
Ozark Valley Mastiffs

99

Your home should be puppy-proofed before bringing home your Mastiff. Even if you think it is safe, there are potential hazards to your pup you may not have even thought of.

Hide or remove any electrical cords within the puppy's reach. Puppies are curious little creatures who love to explore, oftentimes with their mouths. If you cannot remove the cords from your puppy's reach, you may want to invest in some cord protectors. These cord wraps usually come infused with bitter flavors to help deter chewing. If you find you have a particularly stubborn chewer, you can spritz the cords with no-chew spray, found in pet stores, so that he will not find the cord appealing anymore.

Invest in fully enclosed trash cans if you do not have them already. Make sure to keep all trash cans out of reach or locked so that your Mastiff cannot get into it. Even something as small as a cotton swab or a piece of paper may be tempting for him to grab and chew up.

Put up all medications, chemicals, and cleaning supplies. Move all medications and supplements to a high and enclosed location, such as a dedicated medicine cabinet. As mentioned above, puppies explore everything with their mouths, and snatching a bottle or box of medication off the sofa table could prove to be fatal for your new puppy.

Also, chemicals, cleaning supplies, dish pods, and laundry detergent should be placed in an enclosed area and out of reach. This also includes rat bait or poisons that your new puppy may find enticing. Even if you think these items are in an area of the house where your puppy will not be allowed,

Photo Courtesy of Will Fritz

English Mastiffs get very large very quickly and may be able to access areas you previously thought were out of reach.

Watch out for poisonous houseplants. Houseplants may seem innocent, but not all are the same. Some houseplants are actually poisonous and can cause serious issues for a nibbling puppy. Some of the most common houseplants that are potentially dangerous for your new puppy are the corn plant, sago palm, aloe, and jade plant. To find a complete list, visit the ASPCA website.

Beware of xylitol. Xylitol is a sugar alcohol and is commonly found in household items. It is commonly found in chewing gum, mints, candies, toothpaste, and even peanut butter. Xylitol is highly toxic to dogs and can cause dangerously low blood sugar levels resulting in weakness, seizures, trembling, or even death. When dogs consume very high levels of xylitol, it may cause necrosis of the liver, which often leads to death.

Keep all purses and bags, which may contain gum, candies, or toothpaste, up and out of reach of your puppy at all times. Have a designated area for guests' bags so that they are not accidentally left within reach. Also, check all food labels for xylitol before giving your puppy a special treat, especially the pup favorite, peanut butter.

Keep the batteries away. While you probably don't have random batteries lying around on the floor, you may have remotes or small electronic toys. If your puppy is able to get ahold of a battery-operated remote or toy, he could potentially chew them enough to expose the battery. Small button cell batteries are the most dangerous as they are small enough for your puppy to swallow. Swallowing a battery is a serious, life-threatening issue and can cause internal burns. Call the nearest emergency vet immediately if you suspect your puppy may have swallowed a battery.

Put away any children's toys. Children's toys are often made up of small pieces that are a choking hazard to your dog, and many contain batteries too. Be especially careful with toys that contain magnets inside, as these pose an extra risk of internal damage when more than one is consumed.

Set up puppy gates. Your entire home should be puppy-proofed just in case your dog ventures into an area he's not allowed. Once the puppy-proofing is done, however, set up a puppy gate to create a designated "safe zone" for your Mastiff. Use puppy gates to block any doorways or staircases so that it will be easier for you to keep a close eye on him as he adjusts. This will also help with potty training, which will be discussed in greater detail in chapter 6.

It only takes one second for your new English Mastiff to get into something that could cause him harm, so it is extremely important you notify everyone in the house of the changes being made before your puppy comes home.

Dangerous Things Your Dog Might Eat

> "
>
> *I suggest that people who are planning on bringing their puppy home puppy proof their home by keeping all toxic materials, items, and food under lock and key. Keep all electrical cords hidden. Gate off the stairs and the entrance to the bathroom. Make sure you have a variety of new (washed) toys the puppy can chew and play with. Ask the breeder if there is a toy the puppy seems to favor more than another toy.*
>
> **AMBER STEVENS**
> *Glacier's Ridge Mastiffs*
>
> "

Chocolate: Though most humans love it, chocolate is actually very dangerous for dogs. Chocolate contains methylxanthine, which is a stimulant that can stop a dog's metabolic process. Methylxanthines are found in especially high amounts in pure dark chocolate and baker's chocolate. Too much methylxanthine causes seizures and irregular heart function, which can lead to death. If your dog ingests chocolate, call your emergency vet line for help. You may be advised to induce vomiting quickly after ingestion.

Xylitol: As discussed above, xylitol is particularly dangerous to dogs, as it does not take much to cause a dangerous or deadly reaction. Vomiting is typically the initial symptom of xylitol poisoning. If you suspect there is a chance your dog has ingested even a small amount of xylitol, call the veterinarian immediately because time is critical.

Raw or Cooked Bones: Raw or cooked bones are a choking hazard for your dog. The bones can break or splinter and become stuck or, worse, puncture the digestive tract. This is especially true with cooked bones of any kind, as they become dry and brittle. Pork and poultry bones are especially dangerous, as they are more likely to splinter and cause issues.

Though the topic is controversial, some veterinarians say that raw bones of the right variety can provide healthy nutrients and help prevent tartar and plaque buildup in the mouth. Raw bones are recommended only under very close supervision and only for a few minutes at a time. Keep the bone in the refrigerator for a maximum of four days before discarding. If the bone is breaking or if your dog seems to be swallowing any pieces, discard the bone immediately. If you prefer to skip the risk, look for bones in the pet store that are meant to withstand heavy chewing.

Other foods that may cause gastrointestinal upset or worse for your dog are grapes and raisins, certain nuts including macadamia nuts, avocados, apple cores, seeds, and anything in the allium family, including onions and garlic. This is not a comprehensive list, so it is best to check with your veterinarian before giving anything from your plate to your dog.

Preparing an Indoor Space

> *Although your Mastiff is big, he is DELICATE. In approximately two short years, your puppy will grow to be nearly 200 times the size he was when he was born. This means he grows FAST, sometimes upwards of five pounds per week. This also means his bones are fairly soft because they are growing at such an exponential rate. Keep areas with slick floors (hardwood, tile, etc.) blocked off, so the puppy isn't slipping around. Also make sure any stairways or steps are not accessible, to prevent injury.*
>
> **AMANDA GRIFFIN**
> *Gryphon Mastiffs*

Preparing an indoor space for your English Mastiff to safely play and sleep is crucial for keeping him safe and happy when he comes home. Plus, it will make life with a new puppy much easier for you, too.

Crate and Pad: Utilize a crate as a safe space for your Mastiff while you are away or while he is sleeping at night. The crate needs to be large enough to accommodate him at his mature size. Try to find one with a divider that can grow with your pup.

Invest in a quality crate and pad and establish it as a safe place early on in the training process. Washable crate pads are best as they can be cleaned easily. Also, go for low to no stuffing, as it will probably get chewed on at some point. For more information on crates, see Chapter 5.

Puppy Gate or Playpen: Unless your space allows you to keep your puppy contained in a centralized location, you will want to purchase a puppy gate or playpen. This will allow you to create a safe space for your Mastiff so that he can play risk-free without full supervision.

A gate that blocks a doorway is a good way to keep your puppy from venturing down a hall, up the stairs, or into a room that is off-limits. But a

Photo Courtesy of Jessica Olcott

gate still allows the puppy access to furniture and other things that could potentially become chew toys. A playpen allows much more flexibility, as you can move it around wherever inside or outside of the house you will be. A playpen also keeps any furniture from becoming damaged by those razor-sharp puppy teeth.

Preparing an Outdoor Space

Although English Mastiffs do not have high exercise requirements, an outdoor space will help your dog thrive and stay fit and healthy. Preparing an outdoor space and making it pup-friendly is important when it comes to keeping your Mastiff safe. Here's how to do it.

The first thing you need to do is remove all chemical products from the outdoor area, including the garage. Any weed or pest killers, fertilizers,

*Photo Courtesy
of Makayla Tenney*

antifreeze, or other similar products should be placed somewhere the dog cannot reach. Remember, the reach of an English Mastiff is probably further than you think, so make sure such items are tucked away behind a closed door or placed in a locked cabinet.

A secure yard is also crucial for keeping your pup safe. While Mastiffs aren't prone to wandering, they can be prone to digging, and a secure fence is a security feature worth its weight in gold. Check all fencing to be sure there are no gaps between the fence and the ground, and make sure all gates latch completely.

If your Mastiff has a digging habit, there are a few ways you can keep him from tunneling his way out. Burying large rocks halfway in the ground all along the fence line is an effective way to keep him in. `You may also bury your fence in the ground one or two feet. Some people have even had success laying chain-link flat along the ground around the inside fence line to prevent digging.

If you have no fence or your fence isn't secure enough, you can also invest in an electric fence. These fences work by placing transmitters in the ground, dictating the areas where your dog can go. Your Mastiff wears a collar with a small box on it that receives signals when the dog is close to the invisible fence line. If the dog attempts to cross the fence line, he will receive a small shock intended to deter him from continuing. Although this may seem like an affordable alternative to a real fence, these electric fences are known for often failing, especially with large dog breeds who often aren't phased by the shock.

If there is any way for your dog to climb or jump over the fence, remedy that before it becomes an issue as well. Because of the size of this breed, a tall fence, at least six feet, will be required to keep your Mastiff from simply going over it. Also, always be sure your dog is wearing his collar and tags before allowing him outside for any amount of time.

Just like some indoor plants, outdoor plants and flowers can prove to be poisonous to your dog. Check any plants you may have in your garden and replace those that may be harmful with a safe alternative so your curious puppy doesn't accidentally get himself into trouble.

Choosing a Vet

Have a vet chosen for your Mastiff before you bring him home. Most breeders will stipulate a vet visit within the first few days after bringing him home, so schedule that in advance.

The best way to find a reputable vet in your area is to ask around among other dog owners you know. Word of mouth is a great way to get a feel for how a clinic treats patients. You can also check online and read Yelp reviews to make sure you find a good vet.

If you feel more comfortable, call around to multiple vets and ask them any questions you may have before making an appointment. Consider how much experience they have with English Mastiffs, how far they are from home, and how they can be reached in an emergency. Finding a convenient vet office is just as important as finding a reputable one. An excellent vet doesn't do much good in an emergency when you have to drive thirty minutes to get there. You may also want to inquire about cost and compare different offices.

Supplies to Purchase Before You Bring Home Your English Mastiff

Preparing your home isn't the only thing you need to do before take-home day. Making sure you have everything your English Mastiff pup needs before he comes home is essential for a smooth and stress-free homecoming. Follow this list of essentials, and you will have all you need for the day you bring your dog home.

Photo Courtesy of Ashia Cosey

FOOD AND WATER BOWLS

There are so many options when it comes to food and water bowls, from shape to size and even material. These bowls can be made from ceramic, stainless steel, or plastic, but they aren't all created equally. Here's what you need to know before choosing a bowl set for your new puppy.

Plastic: Plastic bowls may come in fun colors and patterns, but they are lightweight, easy to tip over, and many puppies think they are fun to chew on. They are also more difficult to clean when they become scratched or damaged.

Ceramic: Ceramic bowls are heavier, less likely to be tipped over, and are easier to clean than plastic. They are breakable, though, so if your puppy does manage to knock a bowl over, it is likely to chip. With the fast growth rate and the giant size of your English Mastiff, tips and chips are very possible.

Stainless-Steel: Stainless-steel bowls are both easy to clean and unbreakable, so even if a bowl is tipped over and kicked around, it should not be easily damaged. You can also buy these bowls with wide rubber or silicone bases to stop sliding and prevent tipping.

Elevated Bowls: Another option you will find in a pet store is an elevated bowl set. These are bowls that are set up off the floor so that your dog does not have to bend over as far to eat. These were created to try to help prevent the serious issue of bloat in some breeds, but studies have shown that elevated feeders can actually contribute to bloat. Most experts say an elevated feeder is unnecessary and potentially problematic, especially in a giant breed like the English Mastiff. If you are adopting a dog that has neck or mobility issues, then an elevated dog feeder would be something to discuss with your veterinarian as an option. Otherwise, stick to the bowls on ground level for the safest mealtime solution.

Slow Feeder: Slow feeders are bowls with ridges or walls inside designed to keep a dog from eating too quickly. Large breeds are especially prone to bloat, which can occur from eating too fast, making slow feeders a great option.

COLLAR, TAGS, AND LEASH

The collar, tags, and leash are arguably some of the most essential items you should purchase before bringing home your new puppy. These tags are the main way strangers can identify your Mastiff if he ever gets away from you. They can be made at any local pet store, or you can order one from an online retailer. Include your pet's name, your current address, and phone number on the tag. You can even add a little note that reads "Please Call My Family," which may encourage someone to call if they find your lost Mastiff.

FOOD

Your breeder should send a small amount of food home with your puppy to get you through the first couple of days. It's best to continue with this same food as it is probably high-quality and will save your puppy any intestinal upset from switching. If you do switch foods, talk with your breeder about how to do this safely. The breeder will probably recommend you switch the puppy gradually by mixing in his current food with the new food over a period of a few days to avoid tummy troubles.

PUPPY-SAFE TOYS

Your puppy will have lots of energy and very sharp teeth. Unless you want your new boots to become a favorite chew toy, it's probably best to have a few pup-safe toys ready at all times. Get at least one plush toy, one rubber toy or bone, one rope, and one ball. This way, he has a variety and won't get bored and move on to the leg of the couch.

You may even want to buy toys with different squeaker sounds and textures to see which one your puppy will love the most. You may find that plush toys do not last long before being ripped to shreds, or you may find that your new puppy loves carrying that stuffed alligator all around the house!

GROOMING BRUSH

English Mastiffs do not have high grooming needs, but regular baths and brushing will help keep shedding to a minimum. Additional information on grooming will be provided in chapter 12.

PUPPY TRAINING TREATS

Potty training is made much easier with small training treats. Look for soft treats that are healthy and natural. Be sure that they contain no animal by-products, are grain-free, and contain no artificial flavors, colors, or preservatives.

CHAPTER 4

Bringing Home Your English Mastiff

> " Be prepared: your English Mastiff will prefer to sit on your lap most of the time, whether he weighs 50 pounds or 200!
>
> **MELISSA COX**
> *Ozark Valley Mastiffs*
> "

Now that you've done your research, prepared your home, and purchased all the supplies needed to bring your English Mastiff pup home, the time has finally come to pick up your puppy! Follow these tips to make the transition as smooth as possible for both you and your Mastiff.

Picking Up Your English Mastiff

When you arrive to pick up your English Mastiff on that highly anticipated day, your puppy should be waiting for you, either in a playpen alone or with his littermates. No matter how excited you are, be sure to pay attention to all the information given to you by the breeder when you're there. Take notes if you need to.

The breeder should give you detailed information on your puppy's vet records, current shots, future shots, and deworming. He or she should also remind you of any stipulations of the health guarantee and advise you on a feeding schedule. All of this information, as well as breed-specific care tips, should be presented in a packet along with registration papers.

Sometimes a breeder will allow you to take a small blanket or toy home with your dog so that the smell of his litter can comfort him during his transition. It may be beneficial to ask ahead of time if this is an option. You may need to provide the blanket before pick-up day.

*Photo Courtesy
of Angela Brown*

The Ride Home

If you are driving to pick up your Mastiff puppy, it's important to prepare for your trip ahead of time. It is not uncommon for a puppy to get motion sickness and vomit on the ride home, so you might request that the breeder withhold food that morning and take a towel just in case. Be sure to take a bowl and a bottle of water for your puppy, even if the drive is short, in case of an unexpected delay like a flat tire.

There are a few methods of transportation to choose from when traveling in a car with your Mastiff. Some people crate their puppy for the ride home. If you plan to let your new pup travel in a crate, place only towels in the bottom of the crate so that the crate pad is not soiled on the trip. Also, take care to drive smoothly, so you do not jostle your puppy more than necessary.

Photo Courtesy of Fernando Sanchez

When traveling in a crate, make sure the crate is safe for vehicle travel because not all are. Some crates can even become projectiles, potentially injuring you and your pup. Visit the Center for Pet Safety (CPS) website for a list of tested and approved travel crates.

Harnesses and dog seat belts are a great way to travel with your Mastiff, but you should know that they are not all created equally. The Center for Pet Safety performed a harness crashworthiness study in 2013, and results showed that only one of eleven brands tested performed at the level advertised. Some were even deemed "catastrophic failures." Do diligent research on each brand before making your decision, so you can be sure you get a safe one.

FUN FACT
Mayflower Companion?

Records are scarce, but it seems that one or more Mastiffs crossed the Atlantic on the Mayflower with Plymouth colonist John Goodman. A spaniel is also rumored to have been aboard.

Photo Courtesy of Hayley Stangl

Whatever you do, never let your puppy ride in your lap or a passenger's lap. Your puppy could be killed or become a projectile in the event of a crash or even breaking too hard.

Before beginning your journey home, let your puppy relieve himself in the grass and praise him for a job well done. Though he may be nervous, try to make the trip as positive as possible. After all, this is the very beginning of a lifelong journey and companionship for him.

Photo Courtesy
of Ryan & Mary Sackett

The First Night with Your English Mastiff

The first night may seem daunting and uncertain for both you and your Mastiff, and that's okay! This is a transition for all parties that will take adjustment and patience.

Have your puppy's designated sleeping space prepared before your first night together. This should be a crate, at least until your Mastiff is fully potty trained. Many people keep the crate in their own bedroom so they can hear the puppy when he wakes at night, but you can also keep it in a spare room or right outside your door if you are highly sensitive to noise at night. Just be sure you can hear when he wakes so you can take him outside.

When your dog wakes at night, take him outside immediately to his designated potty space. Make this a business trip only with no playtime. Put him right back in the crate when he's done so that he knows it's still bedtime.

Be prepared for a few nights of whining in the crate, as this will be your puppy's first night away from his littermates sleeping alone. If your puppy is having a difficult time sleeping in the crate or keeps you awake with his crying, try talking to your puppy or rubbing his head through the crate to help calm him. The most important thing you can do in the first few days is to make your puppy feel loved and secure. Bonds you form with each other in the early days will last throughout your dog's lifetime, and they will make all aspects of dog ownership more enjoyable.

After a few nights, the bedtime whining should stop, and your puppy should come to find his crate a cozy place to sleep. As you and your puppy adjust to life together, routines will form, and things will fall into place.

The First Vet Visit

As discussed previously, many breeders require you to take your new Mastiff puppy to the vet within a few days of pick-up. Make sure to take all records given to you by the breeder for the vet to include in your Mastiff's file.

The first vet visit should be quick and easy. Your pup will get a general checkup to make sure he is in good health. He will be weighed, and the vet will examine eyes, ears, nose, heart, and lungs. They will look at your dog's skin and coat condition and examine the teeth and mouth. They may take a stool sample to check for parasites. If it is time for your puppy's next round of shots, he will get them at this appointment.

Make sure you take the opportunity to ask the vet any questions you have about caring for your pup. Take a notepad with questions so you don't forget. All in all, the first vet visit should be stress-free for both you and your new English Mastiff puppy.

Photo Courtesy of Andrea Brewing

CHAPTER 5
Being a Puppy Parent

No matter how cute an English Mastiff puppy is, being a puppy parent, in general, is just plain hard. Between cost, training, accidents, and general puppy mischief, your English Mastiff pup will really put you to the test. In this chapter, we'll break down all you need to know to keep your expectations realistic and help you be prepared for real life with a young English Mastiff puppy.

Photo Courtesy of Sabrina Walston

Cost Breakdown for the First Year

The first year with your pup is likely to be more expensive than the average. Between the cost of the pup itself, the initial vet bills and vaccinations, and all the supplies you will need ahead of time, the cost of owning an English Mastiff can really add up.

When searching for an English Mastiff breeder, expect the cost to range anywhere from $1,000 to $4,000 from the most high-quality breeders. As discussed in chapter 2, many breeders will stipulate that you spay or neuter your dog, so prepare for that expense as well, which can cost between $75 and $200.

Though an English Mastiff is a giant dog, due to his sedentary lifestyle, he likely won't eat you out of house and home quite like you may expect. Depending on the type and quality of dog food you buy, it may cost between $800–$1,400 a year.

Between supplies, vet visits, food, and initial purchase price, the cost of owning an English Mastiff can be pretty steep. Because of this, the English Mastiff is not for everyone. If you are not sure how to afford the first year of ownership for your Mastiff, it is probably best you wait until you are certain you can provide him with all he needs before making the commitment.

Having Realistic Expectations

> **"**
>
> *I often tell people to remember that this 25- to 30-pound little bundle of joy will one day be close to 200 pounds, if not more. So, if you do not want a 200-pound dog on your furniture, do not let him get on furniture as a little 20-pound dog, because the habit is very hard to break.*
>
> **TERRY LATVA**
> *North Texas Mastiffs*
>
> **"**

No matter how prepared you are, being a puppy parent is hard. Even the most well-mannered pup will get into some mischief every now and then. So, keep your expectations realistic and the carpet cleaner handy!

Chewing

> Expect for parts of your house to get chewed up so you are mentally prepared and able to act calmly when it does happen. Invest in drool rags and magic erasers (for cleaning slingers off your walls).
>
> **AMANDA GRIFFIN**
> *Gryphon Mastiffs*

Chewing is a universal puppy problem and arguably one of the most frustrating things about being a puppy parent. No matter how much you try to redirect them, those sharp little teeth always seem to find their way into things they shouldn't. As frustrating as it is, chewing is a natural action for puppies as they explore this big, new world.

Instead of scolding or punishing your pup, redirect him with an appropriate chew toy. Never let your Mastiff chew on your hands, no matter how cute it may be when he's tiny. This habit is very difficult to break once it begins.

Your home should be puppy-proofed before your Mastiff arrives, but if you find him still able to reach cords you cannot tuck away, invest in some bitter apple spray deterrent so he doesn't harm himself by chewing through them.

FUN FACT
Long Puppyhood

The English Mastiff has a much longer puppyhood than most other dog breeds. They don't reach mental and physical maturity until they're 3 years old. Exercise should be limited until they're about 2 to help prevent joint problems as they grow.

Chewing due to teething will most likely stop when all your dog's adult teeth have come in, around five to six months of age. However, some dogs chew more than others and will continue the habit into young adulthood. In these cases, it is important to always have a variety of safe and desirable chew toys available to your dog.

*Photo Courtesy
of Ahlex Kortsan*

Digging

Depending on the individual personality of your Mastiff, this breed can be prone to digging. He may dig for fun, he may dig to lie in the cool dirt, or he may, unfortunately, dig under a fence. Though digging can be a dangerous issue, it is also a natural behavior, instinctually driven, and isn't something that should be punished.

If your dog is digging under the fence, address this issue immediately, as this can be dangerous for your pup. Refer to chapter 3 for safe and effective fencing options. If your dog is digging craters in your backyard, try setting up a "dig zone" in the corner where he knows he can dig. Watch him closely and tell him a firm "no" when he attempts to dig outside of the allowed area.

If digging gets out of control, you may need to supervise your pup outside at all times. Reward him for doing his business efficiently with a fun game of fetch. This will keep him occupied and prevent digging.

Barking and Growling

Barking and growling are normal behaviors for pups and typically indicate a playful attitude. Puppies in a litter will play and wrestle with each other instinctually, often barking or growling as they do. This doesn't indicate aggression unless your Mastiff truly appears agitated.

Photo Courtesy of Jessica Olcott

If you want to discourage play fighting, don't do it by punishing your puppy. These are natural behaviors. If your Mastiff begins to play too rough and bark and growl, stop playing immediately and walk away. Come back when the puppy settles down. If your puppy continues to play too rough, repeat the process until your puppy grasps the idea of what is and is not acceptable. This will take time, but it is well worth the effort.

If your Mastiff puppy bites you while playing, make a yelping sound and walk away, ignoring your dog. This is how puppies in a litter indicate that play was too rough. Playful

*Photo Courtesy
of Nikki Tome
Tome Acres English Mastiffs*

behavior that is too rough should not be allowed, as your small pup will quickly grow to a size where accidental injury is possible.

If your dog seems agitated or is biting in a way that seems defensive, it may be time to schedule a trip to see the vet. Truly agitated growling and biting behavior in a previously well-mannered dog can indicate a health problem that may be causing your dog pain.

Separation Anxiety

> *When you first bring your English Mastiff home, he may suffer from separation anxiety from the travel or change of environment. If possible, ask the breeder to send something with a familiar smell with your puppy to help him feel comfortable as he adjusts to his new surroundings.*
>
> **MELISSA COX**
> *Ozark Valley Mastiffs*

Most puppies will whine or bark when left alone. This is normal behavior and will typically stop as the dog becomes accustomed to short spans of time alone. However, a dog with separation anxiety will bark and pace persistently until you return and can often become destructive. Even a house-trained dog may urinate or defecate in the house repeatedly when left alone if he suffers from separation anxiety. In extreme cases, a dog may display signs of coprophagia, a condition when a dog defecates and then consumes his stool.

English Mastiffs are loyal, family-oriented dogs and love to be around their people. These dogs do not do well being left alone for extended periods of time. This giant breed can suffer from separation anxiety if they are not given ample time and attention from their family.

If you cannot commit to spending most of the day with your Mastiff, it may be best to reconsider if this breed is the right one for you. A dog this large, left alone with separation anxiety, can quickly become destructive.

Take your dog for a walk or play a game of fetch just before you leave. This can help tire him out and keep the anxiety at bay. You may also want to leave an interactive toy or puzzle to keep him occupied while you're gone. This can help positively reinforce that being alone can be a treat.

If the separation anxiety is severe and nothing seems to work, make an appointment with your vet to check that there is nothing else going on.

HELPFUL TIP
Puppy Proofing

Even as puppies, Mastiffs are quite large. They can also be mischievous, so you need to puppy proof your home for anything below your waist level.

Crate Training Basics

Though dogs are not true den animals, your pup will still find safety and security in his crate, or "den," in your home. In the wild, dogs and wolves only den when they rear puppies, and the dens are abandoned as soon as the pups are old enough to travel with the pack. Using the crate to create a "den" space in your home can give your Mastiff great comfort.

Though crates can be controversial, the proper use of a crate is actually highly beneficial for both you and your Mastiff. The crate is not merely a cage that contains him; it is a place of rest for him to relax and can even be a great way to house-train.

Types of Crates

There are several types of crates to choose from, including plastic, wire, and heavy-duty crates. The two main types you will find in pet stores are plastic and wire. Most airlines require plastic crates for travel, so if you plan to fly with your dog, be sure your crate is compliant beforehand.

While plastic crates can be lighter weight, wire crates allow for more airflow and visibility for your dog. Wire crates also typically come with a removable divider so you can grow your crate with your puppy. Use the divider while your Mastiff is smaller and gradually make the crate larger as he grows. A wire crate is collapsible and stores and travels easily when the dog isn't using it.

Regardless of which type of crate you choose, make sure it will be large enough for your fully grown English Mastiff, or you may have to buy another larger crate later. Ask your breeder if they can recommend a good brand that works well for an English Mastiff.

Introducing Your Mastiff to the Crate

The key to successful and stress-free crate training is positive reinforcement. If you can reinforce the idea that the crate is a positive place where good and fun things happen, it will go a long way to making it a place he wants to go. Never put your dog in his crate as a form of punishment, as this will send the message that the crate is a bad place. He will be less likely to retreat there for comfort if he associates it with negativity.

Have training treats on hand the first time you introduce your pup to his crate. Begin by securing the crate door to the side of the crate so that it does not bounce around and scare your puppy. Next, place a treat or two outside but near the crate door.

Slowly place the treats closer to the crate until you can put one inside. Your puppy shouldn't fear the crate but should be willing to voluntarily go inside to retrieve the treat. Continue practicing this until you feel your dog is fully comfortable with the crate.

Photo Courtesy of Margie Ullrich

Reward your dog every time he goes into his crate, either with a treat or a special toy. For the first few times, with the exception of bedtime, make crate stays brief. Practice leaving your dog in the crate for about 20 minutes at a time before gradually lengthening it. This will help reinforce the idea that you always come back and can help to ease anxiety. No matter when he last went out, always take your Mastiff to the designated potty area anytime you let him out of his crate.

The crate should always be used humanely and responsibly. Never leave your Mastiff in the crate for extended periods of time, and do not treat the crate like a dog-sitter. If you find your puppy doesn't view the crate as a place of rest, you may want to reevaluate how you use it.

Leaving Your Dog Home Alone

Your dog should be fully comfortable in the crate before you attempt to leave him home alone. Though the first time will probably be nerve-wracking for both you and your Mastiff, if you practice plenty beforehand, he should be both comfortable and safe in the crate while you're gone.

Before leaving your dog for any amount of time, take him on a long walk or play with him intentionally so he can expend his energy. This can help him to relax and hopefully just sleep while you are away. When it's time for him to go into the crate, reward him with a treat just like you did when acclimating him. Give him a "crate only" treat as an additional reward and boredom buster. Interactive treat toys like Kong work great for this.

When you return home, you may be tempted to run and greet your pup with an excited "hello," but this can inadvertently create bad habits. Remember, we want going in the crate to be an exciting time, but coming out of the crate should be calm and no big deal. Open the crate door with little fuss. The crate is a place of calm and safety for your Mastiff, not a place of punishment, so we don't want getting out to feel like a reward.

Crate training takes time and effort. While some dogs take to it quickly and easily, others need more practice. Your Mastiff, naturally, will not like to be left alone, as they are deeply loyal dogs and long for companionship. Be sure not to overuse the crate with your Mastiff, or he may become anxious and lonely. If you intend to leave your dog home for long periods of time while you are away at work, look into dog daycare instead of utilizing the crate.

CHAPTER 6
Potty Training Your English Mastiff

> *Successful house-training is all about repetition. Take your English Mastiff to the same place in the yard every few hours and celebrate every victory with tons of praise!*
>
> **MELISSA COX**
> *Ozark Valley Mastiffs*

Methods of Potty Training

It typically takes between four to six months for a dog to be fully potty trained, but it can sometimes take longer. The goal is to teach your dog that your home is also his home. Instinctually, a dog will not want to soil the places where he eats and sleeps.

When you first bring your English Mastiff home, keep him in a small, confined area of the home to help with potty training. The idea is to not give him enough space to go in a corner and potty. As potty training progresses, give more space at a time.

While potty training, take your dog out often, about every hour. He may not go every time, but reward him with treats and verbal praise when he does. Take him to the same area outside consistently so that he will smell his scent and know it's time to potty. Keep the atmosphere calm while he's doing his business, and don't allow him to play until business is finished.

Though it may take as long as 10-15 minutes, celebrate enthusiastically when your dog does go potty. This will help him associate outside potty time with a rewarding experience. Though it can be frustrating when a dog doesn't catch on immediately, remember that potty training a Mastiff puppy is a process. He wants to please you; he just needs a little time to figure out how.

MY MASTIFF POTTY TRAINING METHOD

by Amanda Griffin – Gryphon Mastiffs

One of the easiest ways to potty train a puppy is to simply pay attention and watch for signals. Make sure your puppy is always where you can see him when he is loose in the house. You may need to use baby gates or to close doors to keep your puppy from wandering off and going potty in the house. When you notice the puppy sniffing around or if you see him start to squat, quickly scoop him up and take him outside.

After the puppy eats or drinks, take him outside to go potty immediately. A puppy will always need to go to the potty shortly after eating or drinking. Control when the puppy eats as well. He does not require a full bowl of food available at all times. He should be fed on a consistent schedule.

When you take the puppy outside after eating or drinking, do not use this time to play. Simply stand or sit off to the side and wait until he finally goes. When he does what he is supposed to and potties, make a HUGE deal out of it. Praise, treats, excitement; make sure he knows he did good. Additionally, every time the puppy goes potty or when you are waiting for him to go, use the word you want to associate with training him to go. For example, you might repeat, "Go potty, good boy! Good potty!" This will train him to understand what you want him to do, which is go potty in the designated spot.

Crate training is also imperative in house-training a puppy, as well as teaching the dog a crate is a good thing. There's nothing worse than trying to crate a 200-pound dog that has never been in a crate before. Choose a crate that is large enough for the puppy to stand and turn around in; never use the crate as punishment, such as a "time out" corner. It should be a place where the puppy feels safe and comfortable.

CONTINUE ▶

Take the puppy outside to go potty before putting him in his crate. He can be safely crated for three to four hours; puppies rarely use the crate as a potty and will learn to hold it while in the crate. Take him outside to potty as soon as you let him out of the crate. While you may feel like you are imprisoning your dog, puppies who are crate trained begin to appreciate the safety and security of their crate, and it becomes a safe place for them. I always give a tiny treat when they go in their crate and eventually turn it into a command the dog knows. When I say 'crate,' the dog goes into the crate. It actually becomes quite handy.

Repetition and consistency are two key factors that will help your puppy learn to let you know he needs to go potty. Whenever you take the puppy outside to go potty, always take him through the same door and to the same area of your yard. This will help to train him to go to that door when he needs to go potty. I have also had luck in making a puppy sit before he goes through any door, anywhere. This teaches the puppy two important things: not to pull you through a door or run out of a door and secondly, to go sit down in front of a door when he wants to go outside. I prefer this to the bell on the doorknob methods because some dogs simply ring the bell incessantly just to go out and play, which can get pretty annoying pretty fast.

If, while training, the puppy does have an accident inside, NEVER punish or scold the puppy unless you catch him in the act. Dogs don't generalize, and if you punish them after the fact, they really don't know what they are in trouble for. Other unacceptable behaviors that have been popular in the past are hitting the dog with a newspaper or rubbing his nose in the accident. These are not productive training methods, and in my personal opinion, would be considered abusive.

On a side note, if you have a dog that has been potty trained for a time and all of a sudden he starts having accidents inside, the first step is a vet visit. The dog could be suffering from a urinary tract or kidney infection and might not be able to control his bodily functions.

Using the Crate for Potty Training

The crate is a great tool to use for potty training because it allows you to control your puppy in a small space during the times you can't supervise him. If you're using a wire crate, install the divider inside while your Mastiff puppy is small so that the accessible area is just big enough for your dog to comfortably stand and turn around in but not big enough that he can take several steps to the other side. This will prevent him from going potty on one side and sleeping on the other.

Not sure how long he should stay in the crate? A good rule of thumb to follow for a young puppy is for every month old he is, that's how many hours he can wait to go potty. That doesn't mean that you should only take your puppy out that often because, if you do, you will most likely be cleaning up a lot of accidents. However, this is a guideline for how long a young puppy can be left in the crate before needing to go out. Never leave your puppy or dog in the crate longer than four to six hours, except at night when every-one is sleeping.

When you wake up in the morning, immediately take your dog outside to the designated potty area. Any delay will most likely end in an accident. Give him however long he needs to go.

Photo Courtesy of Jessica Olcott

If you're planning to put your dog back into the crate while you're gone for work, take the time to exercise him thoroughly before you do. This will help your dog rest better while you're gone. You will need to come home to let your dog out at lunchtime. Follow the same procedure before putting him back into the crate.

If you can't get back home to take your dog out at lunch, you will need to make other arrangements. Doggy daycare is a great option that provides not only additional companionship but also socialization with other dogs. Typically, these places require certain vaccinations, so be sure to call and check ahead of time.

Photo Courtesy of Ashley Burt

If doggy daycare is not an option, call a friend or family member to come by and let your puppy out for you. You can also hire a dog walker to come and exercise your pup while you are away. Go through a reputable service like Care.com so you can read references and know the person has had a background check.

If you absolutely have to leave your dog in the crate or a puppy-proofed room for longer than you should, you can use a puppy pad on one side of the crate. This will slow down the training process because you will, at some point, have to remove the pads and retrain your dog that the only acceptable place to go is outside. If you will be consistently leaving your dog in the crate for extended periods of time, you may need to consider the well-being of your dog and explore other options.

The First Few Weeks

For the first few weeks, take your Mastiff out on a leash, even if you have a fenced backyard. This will help him distinguish the difference between potty time and outside playtime. Remember, he needs to go outside every hour, even during the daytime hours. Early on, he likely won't give you any clues he needs to go out, so take him often anyway.

Remember to praise him heavily when he goes potty outside, especially during the first two weeks. This will help establish the idea that him going potty outside makes you happy.

> 66
>
> *They always pee and almost always poop when they wake up. So be very consistent in taking them out to potty as soon as they wake up from any nap or longer sleep.*
>
> **CLARK HENDERSON**
> *Mystery Mountain Mastiffs*
> 99

Accidents Happen

Accidents in the house are inevitable when potty training, so make sure you have an odor-neutralizing cleaner on hand at all times. Unfortunately, rugs and carpets are typically where most accidents happen because they feel similar to grass under your Mastiff's paws. Take all rugs out while you're potty training if you can, and keep your Mastiff pup contained in an area of the house that has tile or another hard surface until he learns.

If you catch your dog in the act of having an accident in the house, immediately pick him up and take him outside to his potty area. Do not yell or hit your dog, as he is still learning what's expected of him. Many times, accidents in the house happen simply because the owner did not take the puppy out often enough. Sometimes a young puppy will have an accident within minutes of bringing him back inside. Though frustrating,

Photo Courtesy
of Kate O'Brien

Photo Courtesy of Andrea Zimmerman

you still do not want to punish your dog as this will only cause confusion and prolong the process.

Pros and Cons of Doggy Doors

Doggy doors can be very beneficial in your effort to potty train, especially for older dogs. If you have a secure backyard, a doggy door allows your dog to go out to do his business as he feels the urge. This may mean fewer accidents and a shorter training period.

You should never let your dog go outside unsupervised unless you know the backyard is completely secure so your dog cannot get out. (See chapter 3 for more information on how to secure your outdoor space.) Adding a doggy door is not for everyone, though, and there may be several drawbacks. You should review this list of pros and cons before making your decision.

Installation: Installing a doggy door is a permanent change to your home. If you don't own your home, a doggy door is probably not an option for you unless you get it approved by your landlord. In addition, doggy doors are notoriously difficult to install, so make sure you read all the instructions before starting.

Though your English Mastiff may be smaller as a pup, make sure you get a doggy door that is large enough for him when he is fully grown; otherwise, the door will be unusable.

Unwanted Visitors: Unintentional visitors are an unintended consequence of doggy doors. Though they are great for allowing your dog to freely come in and out of your home, they may also offer that same freedom to wild animals.

A doggy door large enough to fit an English Mastiff is unfortunately also large enough for pretty much any animal that may find it or even a human burglar. Be sure to get a locking doggy door that has excellent ratings for keeping unwanted guests out.

Indoor Cats: If you have an indoor cat, it will be nearly impossible to keep him from leaving through the doggy door. If your cat has been declawed, this is particularly dangerous because your cat will have no defense from predators.

If you have an indoor cat who already loves to go outside, a doggy door will allow him to bring his "treasures" inside the house. Finding a dead snake or bird in the house is very likely once your cat discovers how to use the door.

Securing the Yard: Before allowing your English Mastiff to go outside unsupervised, be sure it's a safe area with nothing that could potentially cause him harm. This includes making the fence secure and tall enough and adding a lock to any gate so neighborhood kids or thieves cannot let your dog out. If your dog is a digger, then you may have a problem with him tunneling under the fence. Refer back to chapter 3 to see safe fencing options for an English Mastiff.

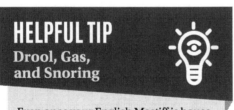

HELPFUL TIP
Drool, Gas, and Snoring

Even once your English Mastiff is house-trained, don't expect your home to be clean and fresh. Mastiffs drool - A LOT - and one shake of their head sends it flying all over your home. Mastiffs are also prone to gassiness, although high-quality food can reduce this issue. English Mastiffs are also prone to snoring.

Backyard Pool: Another danger to consider in the backyard is a pool. Swimming is an activity that many Mastiffs love but not all. Even if your dog enjoys swimming, he should never be allowed near the pool unless you are out there with him.

Swimming alone is dangerous, even for a dog. Allowing full access to the house and pool also permits your dog to

Photo Courtesy of Jessica Rose Big Paw Mastiffs

come in and out freely while wet, causing a big mess for you to clean up when you get home.

If you have a pool, consider a childproof fence to keep your Mastiff out of the water while he's outside.

Fire Escape: One positive to a doggy door is it allows your dog to escape the house in case of an emergency. This could potentially save your dog's life in the event of a fire.

If you know your yard is safe and secure and you want to install a doggy door to aid in training, go ahead! You will still need to confine your dog's indoor privileges to a small space while allowing access to the doggy door. This can be done by using a playpen set up against the wall.

A doggy door is not always a good option, but in the right scenario, it can be very helpful. Though we do not recommend a giant English Mastiff for an elderly owner, for those who have a more difficult time getting around, a doggy door allows the dog to relieve himself in the proper area without any burden to the owner.

CHAPTER 7
Socializing Your English Mastiff

> *To bring out the best in the breed, the key is to socialize, socialize, and socialize. Include the dog in being part of the family with people as well as other animals, both inside and outside the home.*
>
> **CAROL SIMS**
> *Sims English Mastiffs*

Importance of Socialization

English Mastiffs can be naturally wary of strangers and a bit timid. Early and often socialization is the best way to make him feel comfortable around other animals and people. Not only will this help him remain calm in all situations, but it will also make your life easier when you take him out to parks, on walks, or even to a restaurant patio.

Behavior Around Other Dogs

Humans have strict social guidelines to follow when we encounter each other. Dogs also have a set of social rules, though not nearly as strict as ours. Like people, dogs greet a familiar pooch much differently than they do a stranger dog. Much of it depends on the individual dog's personality, but all dogs typically greet each other in one or all of the following ways:

Sniffing: Probably the most notable canine ritual is the sniff test. When dogs greet one another, they may begin with the muzzle or go straight for the backside. Unless one dog seems uncomfortable, this is perfectly normal behavior, and you should allow it to continue until the dogs are acquainted.

Once the dogs have satisfied their sniffers, they can move on to the next step in the canine greeting.

Play Stance: If you see a dog go down into play stance, this behavior is simply one dog attempting to initiate play with another. It's like he's saying, "Hey there! Do you want to be friends and play together?" Even a quick, playful growl accompanied by a friendly tail wag is acceptable.

Again, as long as neither dog seems stressed, there is no need to stop this behavior. Even if the other dog declines the offer to play, that doesn't mean the meeting was negative or not successful.

Exerting Dominance: This particular greeting is probably the least endearing but is still acceptable in the canine world. One dog may exert his dominance by being the first to sniff and by non-aggressively showing the other dog he is in charge. This may even include mounting. This process may be obvious to you, or it may all happen so quickly that you don't even notice until Fido rolls over to show his belly in submission.

As with the other behaviors, these are the natural social ways of dogs and should not be stopped unless there is real aggression or stress. Dogs take social cues well and are pretty good at keeping each other in line. If one is displeased, he will probably let the other dog, and you, know pretty quickly.

Photo Courtesy of Kacey Prentler

> *Make socialization a priority. You need to get your puppy out and about two to three times per week for the first two years and continue regularly past that. Dog parks are dangerous and uncontrolled. Find some local places dogs are allowed (Lowe's, pet stores, feed stores, etc.) that you can take your puppy where there may be a few other dogs, people, etc. You want EVERY experience to be positive. If you are out and about and there is another dog that is acting unruly or barking, remove your puppy from the situation. Never force your puppy to do something he is fearful of. You should also enroll your puppy in a puppy obedience class and continue with lessons until the puppy is a year old. This will teach your puppy to be well behaved around other dogs and focus on you when there are distractions.*
>
> AMANDA GRIFFIN
> *Gryphon Mastiffs*

Safe Ways to Socialize with Other Pets

If you are bringing your Mastiff puppy home to a house with other pets, it will be easier for you to begin the socialization process. Otherwise, you will need to wait until your dog has had his full rounds of vaccinations before you allow him to get close to other dogs. In general, the earlier you can start socialization, the better, as puppies are generally more malleable and willing to befriend others.

It is wise to socialize your Mastiff with the leash on in the early days. This allows you full control if anything goes awry. You may also introduce your dog to another through a fence; however, note that oftentimes dogs can become aggressive when there is a fence between them.

Allow the dogs to meet and greet each other for a few seconds and walk away. Each owner should distract their dog as they are walking away until the dogs are no longer interested in each other. As long as the initial introduction went well, come back and try it again.

Keep the leash loose enough that the dogs can greet each other fully, but not so loose they become tangled, causing stress to the dogs. As the dogs are interacting, read each dog's body language and make sure things remain calm. Bodies should be relaxed, and there should be no staring contests.

As the dogs become accustomed to each other and relaxed, you will be able to let them off-leash to enjoy some supervised playtime with their new pal.

Some trainers believe all first-time dog introductions should be done off-leash so the dogs can behave more naturally. In their opinion, the

Photo Courtesy
of Sabrina Walston

leash becomes a barrier, causing the dogs to naturally be more on edge and defensive. If you choose to introduce the dogs off-leash, do so in a completely neutral area, and make sure both owners are committed to keeping things calm.

A first-time meeting should never be done in one of the dog's yards or home, as this is his territory. This may cause an aggressive or defensive reaction, even if the dogs would otherwise be friendly. It is even more important to monitor the behavior and body language of the dogs while conducting an off-leash meeting. Because off-leash meetings can bring a greater risk, it should only be done between two dogs who are friendly and pre-socialized.

If you are trying to socialize an older Mastiff, be patient and know that this could take much more time. If you have adopted an English Mastiff, you may never know what experiences he has had in the past that could affect his behavior with other dogs going forward. If you need help to socialize an older Mastiff, you may want to call a trainer.

Photo Courtesy of Samantha Davey

Greeting New People

Introducing your Mastiff puppy to new people should be relatively easy as young puppies generally love people and are typically easygoing. The main thing you will want to teach your puppy is not to jump up on new people he meets. It may be cute now, but when he is closer to 200 pounds, it can cause serious injury. If you allow the jumping to continue while he is smaller, the habit will be very hard to break as he grows.

HELPFUL TIP
Gentle Giants

When socialized properly as puppies, English Mastiffs can get along with pretty much any animal and person. They'll cuddle with a kitten or a human child. Without proper socialization as a young puppy, though, they can be aggressive toward other dogs and strangers.

Ideally, your puppy should remain calm and keep all paws on the ground when approached by another person. To stop him from jumping up, teach an alternative command like "sit" so he has something to do instead. See chapter 10 for more information on teaching your dog basic commands.

When your dog gets overly excited and begins to jump, counter with the "sit" command and reward him heavily for staying calm. If he continues to jump, leave the room and ignore your dog for thirty seconds to a minute before coming back in and trying again. This method works when meeting new people, getting the leash out for walks, or any other situation that has your dog jumping for joy.

Introducing an older adopted English Mastiff to new people can be much more of a challenge, as the dog will have a history that is mostly unknown to you. He may have been abused, neglected, or otherwise traumatized, leaving him fearful or even aggressive toward all or some people.

Begin any new human introductions slowly, and allow your dog to lead the way. If he is showing signs of stress, allow him to leave the situation and take a break. Gaining his trust may take time, but it is possible with patience and persistence. If your dog is particularly wary, try separating him and the new people with a baby gate. Have the people ignore him and let him observe without the pressure of being the center of attention.

Once your dog is comfortable around people in general, you may continue socialization in places where he can meet even more new people. Big-box home improvement stores allow dogs and are a great place to take

Photo Courtesy of Jessica Rose Big Paw Mastiffs

your pup to be around others. It's likely many onlookers will stop and ask about the attention-demanding English Mastiff on the end of the leash.

Keep a few small treats available, and reward your dog for any and all positive interactions and good behavior. Remember, early socialization is so important, especially with a giant and protective breed. With enough practice, your English Mastiff can be a well-socialized dog who you can feel good about taking into public spaces.

English Mastiffs and Children

English Mastiffs may be intimidatingly large, but they are surprisingly great with children as long as they are socialized early and often as puppies. Though they are gentle by nature and generally docile, many still suggest only letting them interact with kids under close supervision. This is not because your Mastiff will intentionally cause the kids harm, but because his incredibly large size can be a hazard for small children. One thump of a tail on a face can cause tears and trauma for both a young child and the dog.

It is important you teach your children to be respectful of the dog's space and body, never pulling ears, tail, or other parts. Show them how to gently pet and rub your dog.

No matter how much you trust your English Mastiff, never leave kids alone with your dog unsupervised. This is for the safety of both your Mastiff and the kids.

Photo Courtesy of Nicole Reams

CHAPTER 8
English Mastiffs and Your Other Pets

Introducing Your New Puppy to Existing Pets

> "
> When socializing your Mastiff puppy with other pets, do not allow him to be overly rough or aggressive when playing with other pets. As a puppy, he may be smaller than the pet that he's playing with, but in a matter of a few weeks, the puppy will be bigger. The puppy needs to learn to be gentle. If he becomes overly stimulated and wants to play rough, you can use your 'be nice' voice to try to persuade him not to be so rough.
>
> **AMBER STEVENS**
> *Glacier's Ridge Mastiffs*
> "

Introducing your new Mastiff puppy to existing pets can be easy or difficult, depending on the personality of the animals. As previously mentioned, puppies are generally easygoing and will typically greet new animal friends with excitement. The challenge will be getting your existing pets adjusted to the idea of having a new face around.

English Mastiffs and Other Dogs or Cats

Whether introducing your new Mastiff to a resident dog or cat, begin by bringing home a blanket or a toy with your new pup's scent on it. Let your current pets sniff and become used to the scent before ever introducing them. If you want, you can also take a toy with your current pets' scent on it to the breeder and let the puppy become familiar with it too.

Photo Courtesy
of Rick & Chrissy Moyer

HELPFUL TIP
Socialization is Crucial

English Mastiffs can get along well with other pets as long as they are socialized properly as puppies and introduced to your other pets in the right way. If you bring home an adult English Mastiff, your other pets may be frightened due to their size. With time, everybody should get along well.

If you are introducing your Mastiff pup to another dog, follow the suggestions in the previous chapter. Remember, first meetings should always be done in a neutral place, so your existing pets don't feel territorial.

If you're introducing your Mastiff to a cat, begin by keeping the animals separated but close enough to smell each other. This may be through a gate or even a glass door. After allowing them to get used to each other's presence, try introductions holding your Mastiff pup. If your cat is willing to come close and investigate, do your best to keep your Mastiff calm and reward him for positive interaction.

Your cat can do significant damage to your dog and vice versa, so make sure the first meeting is controlled and safe for all parties. Watch for cat claws and praise both animals for calm interaction.

Most likely, your Mastiff pup will want to play with your cat right away, but your cat may not be too keen. Be sure your cat can always get away to a safe place if he's feeling threatened. This should be an area off the ground that your dog cannot reach.

English Mastiffs and Other Small Pets

Your dog's own personality will determine how he interacts with other small pets, such as rabbits, ferrets, and others. Just like any dog, the English Mastiff can have a strong prey drive, though not always, and may take a liking to chasing small animals. This can, however, be avoided with your own small pets with early and often introductions and socialization.

Also, due to his large size, your Mastiff may cause unintentional harm to small pets by accidentally sitting or stepping on them. If you are nervous about your Mastiff being around your other small pets, keep them separated and do not let them interact.

Photo Courtesy
of Erin Neuman

Introducing an Older English Mastiff

Again, because the history of an older, rescued Mastiff is largely unknown, it is natural that introducing him to existing pets will be more challenging and possibly take more time. Before you adopt an older English Mastiff, ask if you can take him home for a trial run to see if he will get along with your pets. Not all Mastiffs, especially those with traumatic pasts, will do well with other pets in the home. If this is the case, it is best to let the dog go to a home he would be more comfortable in.

Fighting/Bad Behavior

If you find your dogs or other pets fighting or exhibiting bad behavior, it may be time to take a step back and give them space apart from each other. Don't mistake playful fighting and wrestling for true aggression, however, because dogs can often become verbal and rough while playing, even if neither party is agitated.

Handling Aggression

> " Any aggressive behavior directed at either animals or humans can't be tolerated and must be quickly corrected.
>
> **CLARK HENDERSON**
> *Mystery Mountain Mastiffs* "

A well-socialized English Mastiff typically won't have issues with aggression; however, improper treatment can cause a more timid and defensive personality to develop. This is especially important to remember if you're adopting a rescue Mastiff with an unknown past.

If your dog is displaying aggressive behaviors, first try to identify the issue. Is it food and resource aggression? Is your dog territorial over toys or treats? If you can identify a source of aggression, remove it and see if the situation improves.

If it's food aggression, feed your Mastiff alone so he feels comfortable that no one will take his food. If he is particularly possessive over a toy, only allow him to have the toy in the confines of his crate or designated alone

Photo Courtesy of Sondra Swaving

area. Removing your Mastiff from an aggressive situation will not solve the issue, but it can alleviate some stress while you get to the root of the issue.

If your Mastiff is suddenly showing signs of aggression for seemingly no reason, take your dog to the vet to get checked out. Oftentimes, pain and discomfort in your dog can manifest as aggressive behavior.

Also, consider stress factors for your pup. Is he getting enough attention? Is he being left alone for too long? Are any other animals in the house bullying him? An English Mastiff is a highly loyal and loving companion dog and will suffer emotionally if he isn't getting the attention he requires.

As long as your Mastiff isn't causing any harm to you or other members of your household, it should be safe for you to work on carefully socializing the dog more to stop the aggressive behavior. However, if the aggression does not improve or evolves to physical harm in any way, seek a professional trainer's help immediately. Never leave a potentially aggressive dog alone with another animal or person.

> **"**
>
> *If your Mastiff ever starts showing signs of being leery of people, aggressive, or growling, you need to consult a professional positive reinforcement trainer ASAP. Never ever punish a growl. A growl is a warning, and if you punish the warning, it teaches the dog to go straight to a bite.*
>
> **AMANDA GRIFFIN**
> *Gryphon Mastiffs*
> **"**

Raising Multiple Puppies from the Same Litter

There are many reasons why people want to bring home two puppies from the same litter. They may want the built-in companionship of a litter-mate, they may want a dog for each child, or they may simply not be able to choose between two. Regardless of the reason, experts caution against buying two dogs from the same litter.

The work of caring for one puppy is challenging, but two can easily be overwhelming, especially with a giant breed like the Mastiff. Each pup will need to be trained, crated, and socialized separately. Plus, there will be twice the accidents and messes.

Photo Courtesy
of Kristy Banks

Though the dogs will probably grow up as best friends, this relationship often forms at the expense of their human relationships. The dogs often become each other's companions, forming an inseparable bond that the human companions can't compete with.

Most reputable breeders will refuse to sell two dogs from the same litter unless you can provide proof that you can adequately care for them both. Instead, if you want two Mastiff puppies, start with one and plan to get another at a later date. This allows you to give your full attention to training one pup and forming a close relationship before introducing another.

What to Do When Pets Don't Get Along

If you've exhausted all the above tips and your pets simply can't seem to get along, call a professional and get help. Don't hesitate, as the situation could escalate quickly and lead to injury. The sooner you address the aggression with a trained professional, the easier it will be to overcome.

If you find yourself in a situation where you need to break up a fight between dogs, you need to know how to do so safely so that you are not harmed in the process. Use the wheelbarrow method by grabbing each dog by the back legs and pulling them apart. You will need two people restraining the dogs for this method.

If you are alone, grab two metal pots and bang them against each other to make a loud noise. This should startle and distract the dogs long enough for you to separate them before the aggression continues. Water also works well to distract them. If you are outside, grab the hose and spray both dogs to distract them so you can separate them physically.

Never put yourself between two fighting dogs, no matter how much you trust them. This could likely lead to injury, especially with the large size and brute strength of the English Mastiff, even if he does not intend to cause you harm.

CHAPTER 9

Exercising Your English Mastiff – Physically and Mentally

Exercise Requirements

> *Mastiffs are such laid-back dogs, even as puppies. I always tell folks that because of their fast growth rate, they tire easily, so don't walk them any further than you can physically carry them home! Oftentimes they will just lie down as if to say: 'I'm too tired to go any further. I'll just nap right here.*
>
> **TERRY LATVA**
> *North Texas Mastiffs*

Despite their colossal size, English Mastiffs have relatively low exercise requirements for their size and muscular build. Just like all dogs, Mastiffs do need daily exercise to stay fit and healthy, but a 20- to 30-minute daily walk should suffice. Be sure not to take a Mastiff any further from home than you are willing to carry him as they are notorious for simply lying down and relaxing whenever and wherever they get tired, even if it's in the middle of the sidewalk!

English Mastiffs also benefit greatly from active play at home if a walk isn't possible. Surprisingly, these dogs do very well in an apartment setting as long as they get their activity in.

Types of Exercise and How to Make it Fun

> *Adult Mastiff energy levels can vary. Some need quite a bit of exercise, while others are really couch potatoes. The main thing to remember is to give them enough exercise to keep them at a healthy weight. If they are full of energy, they need to burn it through exercise. If they are a bit lazy, then they probably just need a walk routine to keep them fit.*
>
> **CLARK HENDERSON**
> *Mystery Mountain Mastiffs*

A simple walk around the block is a great way to get your Mastiff active, but that can become mundane and is dependent on good weather. Since the English Mastiff is not a particularly athletic breed and doesn't do well in sports or agility, you may be wondering how to make exercise more fun for the both of you. This section will cover additional ways to exercise your dog that are fun, exciting, and can even be done indoors on a rainy day.

Flirt Pole: A flirt pole is a stick with a toy attached by a string. This is one of the best ways to exercise your dog if you are disabled, as you can use it from a seated position. To use a flirt pole, simply drag the toy on the ground in a circle or across the yard and watch your Mastiff try to catch it as it moves. Not only is this great physical activity, but it keeps your dog mentally engaged too.

Photo Courtesy of Kristy Banks

Hide and Seek: This is a great indoor game to play with your Mastiff after he has mastered the "sit" and "stay" commands detailed in chapter 10. Take your dog to a place in the house and have him sit and stay there while you go hide. Once you have found a hiding spot, call to him and let him find you!

If he has trouble staying still long enough for you to hide, try giving him a treat that takes him a minute or so to finish, then call to him when he's done. Keep calling him periodically to give him hints until he finds you. This game is fun for you and him and is the perfect indoor activity for a rainy or cold day.

Fetch: A classic game of fetch is always an excellent way to get a dog moving. Grab a ball, rope, Frisbee, or anything else you can find and start throwing. Teach your dog to return the item to you and watch him tire himself out while having a blast in the process.

Scavenger Hunt: Your English Mastiff has a powerful sniffer with up to 300 million olfactory receptors in his nose. Not only that, but the part of his brain dedicated to smelling is proportionally 40 times larger than a human's. That's some keen smell power!

Make mealtime or snack time a game with a scavenger hunt and put that nose to the test. Hide small amounts of food or treats throughout a room and see if your Mastiff can sniff them out. This may not be a lot of exercise for your dog, but it's a great way to get him stimulated on a slow day. Just

Photo Courtesy of Rose Nelson

be sure you remember where you hid the food so you don't end up with ants later!

Doggy Daycare: A local doggy daycare is a fantastic outlet for your dog to not only get out his energy but also to get more socialization with other dogs. This is a great alternative to leaving your dog home all day if you need to be out. After a few hours of daycare, your Mastiff will be ready for a nap, no doubt.

HELPFUL TIP
Lonely Couch Potatoes

Mastiffs don't need a ton of exercise, but they should get a 30-minute walk daily to maintain joint mobility and prevent obesity. English Mastiffs do tend to get extremely attached to their people and are prone to separation anxiety. Leave them with puzzle toys and other enrichment to keep them busy when you're gone.

Playdates: Playdates are another great way to exercise your Mastiff. Just like with doggy daycare, playdates with familiar dogs can help your dog continuously improve his social skills, as well as keep him mentally stimulated. Meet a dog friend or two at a local dog park and let them play away. Don't have dog friends? Introduce yourself to people you meet at the dog park and make new ones.

Exercise Requirements by Age

A fully grown English Mastiff has very different exercise requirements than a puppy or a senior dog. Be very careful when exercising young puppies, as they are still growing and may be more vulnerable to injury, especially to the growth plates. A Mastiff actually takes longer than most dogs to mature. The injury risk wanes around the age of 24–36 months, but until then, exercise should remain low impact, no matter how energetic your Mastiff puppy seems.

The same basic rules apply to senior dogs that are, by nature, prone to more injury. When your dog reaches his senior years, keep the exercise consistent but low impact. Slow walks are perfect for senior dogs. Avoid any climbing or jumping. Swimming is an excellent option for senior dogs, as it is good exercise and has almost no impact.

If your senior dog begins to limp after exercise, see your vet about possible arthritis. This is a common condition that can typically be managed with the right care.

The Importance of Mental Exercise

Mental exercise is equally as important as physical exercise. A bored or lonely dog can become a destructive dog, and a 200-pound destructive dog can do quite a bit of damage. As mentioned previously, English Mastiffs are very family-oriented. If your lifestyle prohibits you from spending enough time with or giving your dog enough mental stimulation, consider a different breed.

Tips for Keeping Your English Mastiff Occupied

One of the easiest ways to challenge your dog's mind is with a dog puzzle or an interactive toy. The Trixie Poker Box is a dog puzzle that has four compartments covered by a lid. It's your dog's job to figure out how each

*Photo Courtesy
of Amber Sawyer*

Photo Courtesy of Kara Kamotzki

lid can be removed to get to the reward waiting inside. All four lids open differently, so this will take some real focus and determination on your dog's part.

Kong makes a range of interactive toys that will keep your dog occupied for a long time. These toys are made of rubber and are basically indestructible, which is important for a breed like the English Mastiff. Stuff the toys with Kong treats or simply use peanut butter and watch your dog go crazy figuring out how to get the goodies out.

Teaching your Mastiff a new command is another great way to get his brain going and keep him sharp. Once he's mastered the basic commands, move on to more exciting and challenging tricks like jumping through a hula hoop or playing dead. The more you work with your dog on obedience, the closer your bond becomes and the more willing and obedient he will naturally be.

Additionally, there are electronic toys that can be used to entertain your Mastiff while you are busy or away. Clever Pet is a unique system that challenges your dog with sequences, memory games, and electronically released treats or food when solved. This system comes with a light-up pad that shows different colors and patterns. Clever Pet is designed to progressively get more challenging as your dog figures it out.

You can monitor use and track your dog's progress using a mobile app. This system is great for dogs left home alone for any period of time. It is pricey, at about $250, but it may be worth it for a dog that has to consistently spend time alone. Just remember, this toy is not a substitute for quality time spent with you.

Photo Courtesy of Kelly Lowe

Toy rotation is another way to keep your Mastiff on his toes. Swap out his toys every week or two, so he's always interested and engaged.

CHAPTER 10
Training Your English Mastiff

> *Mastiffs are very intelligent dogs and easy to train with consistent, positive reinforcement. Your Mastiff wants nothing more than to make you happy, so praise him every chance you get!*
>
> MELISSA COX
> *Ozark Valley Mastiffs*

Benefits of Proper Training

Not only does proper training make life with a giant breed easier, but it provides a level of safety that is immeasurable in worth and will grow your bond with your dog deeper than you thought possible. A properly trained English Mastiff will come when called and can be trusted in public no matter what situation arises. Knowing that you can trust your dog to obey in an emergency will give you peace of mind and may even save his life.

English Mastiffs are intelligent dogs but are known to be stubborn at times. Keeping training sessions short and engaging can make it easier for your dog and you. If your Mastiff feels confused or senses that you are becoming frustrated, he may shut down, and it will become impossible to make progress. Positive interaction and reinforcement are key to successfully training a Mastiff.

> *They are actually really intelligent dogs; they were just bred to think for themselves and not 'take orders,' so sometimes their stubbornness comes off as stupidity when it's really just stubbornness.*
>
> **AMANDA GRIFFIN**
> *Gryphon Mastiffs*

Training Your English Mastiff at Home

Training at home can be done either by you or by a professional trainer that comes to your home. There are both benefits and drawbacks to training your English Mastiff at home. One benefit is that your Mastiff will feel comfortable and safe in a familiar environment and be able to focus on the training without the distraction of new surroundings or other dogs.

If you choose to train your Mastiff yourself, you and your dog will learn to trust each other in a beautiful way. Training at home is also beneficial in the early days when your Mastiff is still too young to go out to public places or training facilities.

One drawback of training at home, either by yourself or with a personal trainer, is that your dog will only be learning these commands in a calm, familiar environment. This can be an issue if your dog refuses to obey when there are real-world distractions around. This problem can be overcome by practicing obedience outside with distractions, even on a balcony if you're in an apartment. When your dog is old enough to go to public spaces, take him to a park and practice obedience to train him in less than ideal conditions as well.

Photo Courtesy of Kaylee Jarrell

No matter how you train at home, make sure you keep the sessions positive, practice obedience in a variety of settings, and focus on your bond for an optimal experience and result.

> *From my experience, Mastiffs are not always impressed with repetition. So the key to success in training your Mastiff is to keep him interested in what you are teaching by doing less repetition, more often, with great rewards. It pays off in the end.*
>
> **AMBER STEVENS**
> *Glacier's Ridge Mastiffs*

Methods of Training

There are two mainstream methods of training, which are hotly debated among experts. One is known as alpha-dog training, and the other is positive reinforcement. Before choosing a method of training for your Mastiff, it's important that you fully understand the details of each.

Alpha-Dog Training: You may recognize the alpha-dog training method popularized by television dog trainer Cesar Millan. This method of training focuses heavily on maintaining total control over your dog and his actions. Alpha-dog training teaches that you should never allow your dog in your bed, never allow your dog to go through a doorway before you do, and never get down on eye level with him.

Proponents of this method claim that because dogs are pack animals, they need a clear leader and "alpha" in order to learn to submit. They believe because wolves exert their dominance over each other to keep the pack in check, they attempt to do the same, even by using highly controversial methods. Research has actually shown that wolves in the wild do not have such a rigid hierarchy, and instead, they live very socially among each other, much like human families.

Alpha training employs the use of restraints such as shock collars, choke collars, and forceful body maneuvers.

HELPFUL TIP
Early Training is Critical

It's tempting to let your English Mastiff puppy get away with anything. However, you need to remember they may outweigh you as an adult. Leash walking, in particular, must be mastered while your Mastiff is still small. Whatever rules you intend to implement on your adult Mastiff – like staying off the furniture – must be imposed right away with your puppy.

*Photo Courtesy
of Makayla Tenney*

Rather than positive reinforcement, this method relies on punishing your dog for what he is doing wrong rather than taking the time to redirect him to the right action or behavior. While some believe alpha training is effective, others believe it is cruel and causes fear, undermining your relationship with your dog.

> 66
>
> *Mastiffs love to please their owners. Sometimes it takes them a little longer to pick things up, but once they do, I swear they would climb a tree if you asked them to! As long as you have patience, they will eventually understand all that you're asking of them. Just be fair and consistent. Mastiffs are very food driven, so treats go a long way in the training process!*
>
> **TERRY LATVA**
> *North Texas Mastiffs*
>
> 99

Positive Reinforcement

Positive reinforcement is the most widely used method of training today. This method reinforces good behavior and obedience with treats and praise, encouraging a positive relationship between trainer and dog while also teaching expected behavior. It is still important to establish dominance and control in the relationship; however, this is done through positive reinforcement rather than force. Improper behavior is redirected rather than punished.

Your English Mastiff will want to please you and craves your companionship. Using positive reinforcement to train your Mastiff will help him understand what you want him to do. This is essentially the opposite of fear-based training and will build loyalty and trust instead.

HELPFUL TIP
Easy to Train as Long as You're Gentle

Since Mastiffs love their people so much, they are usually easy to train with positive reinforcement. However, they are very sensitive dogs. Punishing them can cause fear aggression, so always be gentle when training your English Mastiff.

There are two types of positive reinforcements used, primary and secondary.

Primary Reinforcement: Primary reinforcements are directly related to the basic needs of your dog. These are things like food and water. This does not mean food and water are withheld until obedience is achieved; rather it employs extra rewards like food and training treats as primary reinforcements. Treats made specifically for training are small so that your dog can train longer without being overfed. Some trainers also use small bits of deli meat as a highly desirable primary reinforcement.

Secondary Reinforcement: Secondary reinforcements are things not based on basic needs but rather on learned social constructs. These things include verbal praise, smiles, pats, and anything else your dog has learned means you're pleased.

There is a secondary type of secondary reinforcement called conditioned reinforcement. This includes otherwise neutral sounds and objects like a clicker or whistle. When used in conjunction with primary reinforcements, these objects become positive by association. Conditioned reinforcement can be effective initially but can lose effectiveness when the primary reinforcement is taken away.

> 66
>
> *Mastiffs have a strong desire to please. Encourage them with treats, but always include praise.*
>
> **SHARON JOHNSON**
> *Johnson Farms Mastiffs*
>
> 99

Dangers of Negative Reinforcement

Correcting by punishment, as done in alpha training, can lead to anxiety, fear, and even aggression in your dog. This method has no research-based proven effectiveness. Using this method without a trained professional can lead to a damaged relationship with your dog and a permanent loss of trust.

When you punish your dog for doing something wrong, he will become confused and unsure of how to please you. He may never even fully understand what action was the reason for his punishment and discomfort in the first place. This can lead to frustration for all parties and potentially put you and your family in danger. Showing your dog what he should be doing rather than what he shouldn't may take a bit longer, but it is worth it to watch your relationship grow positively.

> "
>
> *Most Mastiffs are very easy to train because of their willingness to please their owners. They are a 'soft' breed, meaning they require little to no scolding. A simple raised voice may have a reaction similar to that of a much worse punishment. I can give my Mastiffs a look and point my finger and they act like I've punished them for days. Positive reinforcement training methods are really the only way to go with a Mastiff. Praise and treats every time he does something correct or that you are happy with, and he will learn quite quickly.*
>
> AMANDA GRIFFIN
> *Gryphon Mastiffs*
>
> "

Basic Commands

Teaching your Mastiff basic obedience and commands isn't only about learning to sit or shake. It's equally about building trust between you and your Mastiff and learning to communicate with each other.

Most obedience classes or trainers will begin the session by teaching a few basic commands. These will lay the foundation for more complicated commands later. If you are choosing to train your English Mastiff yourself, follow the steps below to help him master five basic commands.

FUN FACT
Varied Careers Over the Years

English Mastiffs and their Molosser ancestors have worked a variety of jobs over the years. They fought in wars around Asia and Europe. They battled gladiators in Roman colosseums. They protected the homes of British aristocrats. They were used in bull- and bear-baiting. Then, they were transformed from fighting dogs to friendly family pets.

Sit: The sit command is the easiest one to teach and can be learned in a short period of

Photo Courtesy of Ashlyn Mathews

time. Take your dog to a calm area, free of distractions like toys, and have small training treats ready.

With your dog standing and facing you, hold a treat in front of his nose and slowly raise it up and over his head so he is forced to sit down and look up. Give the verbal command "sit" as you do this. When he sits, reward him with a treat and a key phrase such as "yes" or "good." If you're training with a clicker, also give a click when he obeys the command.

Down: Have your Mastiff sit facing you. Hold a treat in front of his nose, lower it to the floor, and give the verbal command "down." If your dog raises his backside to a standing position to retrieve the treat, take the treat away and say "no." Begin again from a seated position. When your dog success- fully lies down to retrieve the treat, reward with a treat, a positive verbal cue such as "yes," and a click.

Heel: Teaching your dog to heel requires him to walk on your left side at your pace whenever you're out and about. The heel command is a bit challenging and requires significant focus from your dog. He must stop when you stop and walk when you walk, never stepping in front of your left heel. This command is great for preventing leash tugging, which is especially important with a giant breed like the Mastiff.

Begin by having your dog sit in front, facing you. Using your left hand, let your dog smell the treat and then swing your arm around to the left, luring your dog to turn around and stop in a position next to you but slightly behind, facing the same direction you are. Reward your dog immediately when he arrives in the correct position. Use the command "heel." Repeat this command many times, always having your dog come to the heel position before rewarding him.

After your dog has mastered the heel position, progress by taking a few steps using the same verbal "heel" command. Reward your dog for walking with you in the correct position. If your dog leaves the correct heel position, guide him back to where he is supposed to be before continuing.

Stay: To teach your dog to stay, command him to sit, facing you. With a visible treat in hand, hold up your palm to your dog and say, "stay." Take one step back. If your dog doesn't move, quickly return and reward him.

You don't want him leaving the stay position to retrieve the treat. If your dog moves, say "no" and return him to a sitting position. As your dog gets the hang of "stay," increase the number of steps you walk away.

Leave It: This command is valuable and can help keep your dog safe if he gets into something potentially dangerous. Begin with two treats, one in each hand. Keep one hand in a fist but allow your dog to sniff the treat. As your dog tries to get into your hand to get the treat, verbally command him to "leave it." Repeat this command until your dog backs off and then reward with the treat from the other hand. As your dog progresses, make the treat more accessible and challenge your pup to leave it in exchange for another treat.

When to Hire a Trainer

If you choose to train your Mastiff at home and are unable to make progress or accomplish basic obedience, consider hiring a trainer. Training a dog is challenging and takes a great amount of time and consistency. Proper and early training is so important, especially with a dog as large as the English Mastiff. You do not want to allow him to get big enough to overpower you before you've mastered some obedience training.

If you're dealing with any kind of aggression or persistent bad behaviors, seek professional help immediately before the issue escalates.

CHAPTER 11

Traveling with Your English Mastiff

> *Mastiffs do not always make great travel companions because they take up an entire back seat of your vehicle. But if you have room in the vehicle that you're using for your Mastiff, they make wonderful companions. If you are planning on staying in a hotel, check in advance for their pet policy to make sure their rooms can accommodate your Mastiff.*
>
> **AMBER STEVENS**
> *Glacier's Ridge Mastiffs*

Traveling with your Mastiff may seem like a good idea, but it can put unneeded stress on your dog. This chapter will guide you through all that traveling with your dog entails so that you can make the best decision for you and your Mastiff.

Flying with Your Dog

Flying with a dog as large as an English Mastiff can be a challenge. With his giant size, your Mastiff will always be forced to ride in the cargo area in a crate, which can be traumatizing for some animals. In the past, airlines often treated animals like luggage, and they weren't always properly cared for. Some even died due to high or low temperatures. Though airlines have begun enforcing regulations to keep traveling animals safe, it can still be a scary experience for your dog.

While airlines vary on their rules and regulations for pet travel, most charge a fee for animal transport. This can cost anywhere from $75–$200

Photo Courtesy
of Jennifer Tapscott

HELPFUL TIP
Hotel Cautions

Some hotels don't allow dogs at all, and many hotels that do allow dogs have a maximum weight limit. When traveling with your English Mastiff, always call hotels ahead of time to make sure your gentle giant will be allowed to stay with you.

each way. If you do choose to fly with your Mastiff, try to get a direct flight so that your dog only has to go through the experience once each way. Also, many airlines offer limited spots for pets, so book early.

Some airlines require a certificate of veterinary inspection (CVI) before flying. Also keep in mind, federal regulations prohibit any pets under eight weeks from flying.

The International Air Transport Association (IATA) specifies guidelines for approved kennels, which have been accepted by most airlines. These guidelines change, so check recent regulations before your flight to make sure your kennel is approved by your specific airline. Choosing a safe and approved crate for your Mastiff to fly in is one of the most important decisions you will make traveling with him.

If you choose to fly with your Mastiff, there are a few basic care specifics you need to know before you go. Most airlines will allow you to attach a bag of food that may be used in case of delay. Some even allow a drip water dispenser for your Mastiff on the flight, so it's important you let your dog practice with one of these before the flight if he is unfamiliar.

Many airlines will also allow a small blanket or piece of clothing in the crate with your scent to bring him comfort, but typically ban crate pads, toys, bones or treats, newspaper, straw, or hay bedding. Most also do not allow any collar other than a flat collar. Muzzles, shock collars, and metal collars are prohibited. Sending medication with your dog is also not allowed. Because each airline is different, confirm with your specific airline before you plan.

Your Mastiff will have to be checked-in in his kennel with the cargo, so make sure you arrive as late as possible and take him outside to relieve himself just before entering the airport. Know where you can take him out ahead of time, as grass is often hard to find once you enter the airport property. Stopping at a nearby gas station just before you get there may be a good option. It is wise to withhold food and limit water for several hours before travel so that your dog does not become sick or need to relieve himself on the flight.

Emotional Support Dogs

Until a recent FAA rule change, it was possible for your dog to fly in the cabin with you as long as he was registered as an emotional support dog. This simply required a letter to the airline in advance of the flight. Recent rule changes have deemed that only certified service dogs performing a task or benefit for a disabled person will be allowed in the cabin during a flight. This means emotional support dogs no longer qualify as service dogs on airplanes.

Photo Courtesy
of Nikki Whitmore

Photo Courtesy of Kate Collazo

Hotel Stays

Before planning overnight travel with your Mastiff, make sure you have hotel arrangements ahead of time if needed. Not all hotels are pet friendly, and even those that claim to be may have breed and size restrictions. Before booking, call and check their pet policy and make sure they will allow a dog as large as a Mastiff.

Another thing to consider when choosing a hotel is whether or not it has adequate outdoor space. Even some "pet friendly" hotels aren't actually convenient for pets, as there is no space to walk your dog or let him do his business. Be sure to request a room on the ground floor so that you don't have to take the stairs or elevator every time your dog needs to go outside.

Some hotels reserve old, outdated rooms for pets, so call and check ahead of time if the pet rooms are different from the other rooms. Even if you don't anticipate using it, bring a kennel to the hotel in case you have to leave your dog unattended. You never know when an emergency will happen, and it's better to be prepared.

These same principles apply to Airbnb and VRBO rentals as well. Double-check that a property is Mastiff-friendly and has adequate accommodations and outdoor space before you book.

Kenneling vs. Dog Sitters

If you opt to leave your dog home while you travel, there are two basic care choices for him. You can leave your dog at a boarding facility, or you can hire a dog sitter. Depending on how long you will be gone and your dog's specific personality, either of these can be good care options. If you have responsible family or friends around, you could also recruit them to care for your loyal Mastiff while you're away.

If you're planning a short trip, a dog sitter may be a more affordable option. Typically, a dog sitter will come by your home and take your dog out two to three times a day and make sure he has food and water. You can check care.com for a reputable and trustworthy dog sitter or ask a family member or friend that you trust. Because the English Mastiff needs companionship and will suffer if left alone, this is only an option for a day or two. After this, he may become anxious and destructive.

If you hire a dog sitter, be sure they have experience with a giant breed like the Mastiff. Otherwise, they may be easily overwhelmed or overpowered by his size and strength on the leash. Some dog sitters will stay overnight to care for your dog. This is a pricier option but is better for your Mastiff, as he won't be alone.

Choosing the Right Boarding Facility

If you're planning an extended trip away, take your Mastiff to a boarding facility instead. This will allow him to have constant companionship and care. These facilities also allow your dog socialization and playtime with other dogs. Be sure your dog is properly socialized and accustomed to playing with other dogs before taking him to a boarding facility. If he doesn't play well with others, he may be forced to remain in his kennel for the majority of the time.

Photo Courtesy of Kimberley Thompson

If your Mastiff is well trained and socialized, a stay at a boarding facility will be like a vacation for your dog!

Photo Courtesy
of Rose Nelson

Every boarding facility is different and enforces its own unique rules and policies. The accommodations range from basic kennels to full-sized rooms with elevated dog beds and doggy doors to a private patio. Frequently, quality boarding facilities will have a common area inside and out where dogs can play and romp. The cost per night varies greatly depending on location and amenities.

Every quality kennel will require a Bordetella vaccine before your dog's stay. Never take your dog to a place that doesn't. Bordetella is highly contagious and common, and it only takes one dog to cause an outbreak that makes your dog sick. Plan for your dog to get the vaccine a minimum of two weeks before his stay.

Ask around among other dog owners and check reviews before you choose a place to take your dog while you're away. You don't want to take your beloved Mastiff just anywhere. Be sure they can provide adequate care and interaction before you pick.

Tips and Tricks for Traveling

Traveling with your Mastiff can undoubtedly be as stressful as it is fun. Follow these helpful tips and tricks for a smooth sailing trip.

- Don't feed your dog within four hours of any trip, including short car rides. Otherwise, you may be cleaning up vomit when your Mastiff gets sick in the car.

- If you know your Mastiff will be taking a long trip, give him a little more exercise than normal the day before. This can help wear him out, so he sleeps and relaxes on the trip.

- Do not sedate your dog. This practice was common at one time but is no longer recommended. Sedation can make your dog sluggish and inhibit him from reacting in an emergency. Plus, it is simply bad for his health.

- If flying, check-in as late as possible so that you don't have to leave your dog waiting alone for hours before take-off.

- Check that all rental cars and hotels accept pets before you arrive.

- Always have water and a bowl on hand, plastic bags for waste, and a leash ready. No matter your method of transportation, these items are basic necessities.

- Always have the number of a vet local to your current location in case of an emergency. Things can happen anywhere, so be prepared.

No matter how you plan to travel, the key to success is planning ahead of time so that there are no surprises for you or your dog. Double-check all arrangements just to be sure it's all going to go according to plan!

CHAPTER 12
Grooming Your English Mastiff

Coat Basics

> *A Mastiff owner can expect a Mastiff to blow his coat out twice a year. Mastiffs can have a double coat and/or a tighter finer coat. These two different coat types determine the amount the dog will shed. I've noticed that they tend to shed less based on the quality of their dog food; the higher the quality, the less shedding I notice. Using a Furminator once a week also helps with removing the dead hair.*
>
> **AMBER STEVENS**
> *Glacier's Ridge Mastiffs*

The English Mastiff possesses a short, straight outer coat with a dense short undercoat, which comes in fawn, apricot, or brindle. Their coats are fairly easy to care for and require little maintenance. This breed sheds year-round, especially in the spring and fall, so coat care will revolve around keeping your dog's coat healthy and minimizing shedding.

Basic Grooming Tools

> 66
>
> *I love to use a vacuum (Shop-Vac) on my dogs as it does a great job of removing the undercoat, and the dogs love the feeling of the cool air vacuuming their coats. I recommend starting when you get your puppy at eight weeks as he will learn to love it!*
>
> **TERRY LATVA**
> *North Texas Mastiffs*
>
> 99

For the English Mastiff's low-maintenance coat, you will only need a few tools to get you through. Begin with a good shampoo and coat conditioner. Check with your vet to see which brand they recommend, or check reviews online to find a quality brand. Never use human shampoo on your dog.

You will also need something to brush your dog with. Choose between a rubber hand mitt and bristle brush, which will help finish and shine your dog's coat. Get your dog used to these tools as a young pup, even before he needs them so that he is comfortable with them. This will make it much easier for you to care for his coat.

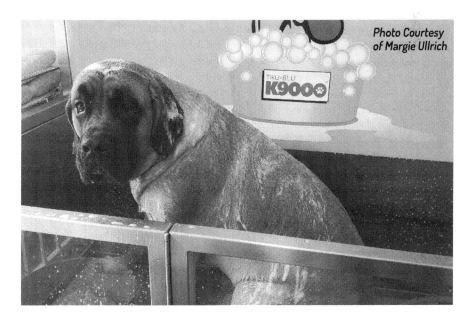

Photo Courtesy of Margie Ullrich

Photo Courtesy of Kate Collazo

Bathing and Brushing

An occasional bath is all your Mastiff will need to remain clean and keep his coat healthy. In fact, too frequent baths can be drying for your dog's skin. Unless he gets dirty while playing outside, aim to bathe him no more than once every two months or so.

The choice of shampoo is largely a personal preference. Whichever you choose, make sure it is free of parabens, dyes, sulfates, and DEA. These ingredients are common in commercial shampoos but are damaging to your dog's health over time. It is also best to avoid fragrances, as they can irritate your Mastiff's skin.

Bathe your dog in the shower or tub with a hand sprayer if possible. With his large size, it will be challenging to rinse the shampoo out of his fur with a cup. Be sure to clean your Mastiff's coat all the way down to the skin. Rinse with cool water, then use a towel to dry him.

Because your Mastiff's coat is so short, he will dry quickly and likely won't need to be blow-dried. If you want to go ahead and use the blow dryer to dry him even faster, make sure you hold it far enough away not to burn him.

When it comes to brushing, begin with either a bristle brush or a rubber hand mitt. If your dog is shedding a lot, a metal comb or a de-shedding tool can help to ease the problem. Use these weekly or more as needed to prevent heavy shedding. Never shave your Mastiff, as his coat helps regulate his body temperature.

Photo Courtesy
of Rick & Chrissy Moyer

Nail Trimming

Some Mastiff owners prefer to have a vet or groomer trim their dog's nails, but this is something you can easily do at home with a quality nail trimmer. There are several types of nail trimmers, but what you choose should be based on preference, as they are all effective. You will also need to have styptic powder on hand to stop the bleeding just in case you accidentally cut into the quick.

HELPFUL TIP
Wrinkle Care

A Mastiff's wrinkles are adorable, but they need a little extra care. Use a damp cloth or unscented baby wipe to clean out the wrinkles daily, then towel dry the area well. Wrinkles are prone to skin infections, so do your best to keep them clean and dry.

A dog's nail is made up of two parts, the nail and the quick. The quick is the pink part inside the nail where the blood vessels are. In light-colored nails, the quick may be visible, making it easy to avoid, but that is not the case for dark nails. Quicking, or cutting into the quick, is a very painful experience, so trim nails a small amount and repeat in several days if they are still too long.

The most common types of nail clippers are the scissor type and the guillotine type. Read directions included with each for proper use. Here's a basic how-to for either type.

1. Place your Mastiff's nail in the clipper and cut away from the pad at a 45-degree angle.
2. If you're trimming extra long nails, take it only a little at a time, as the quick will retreat as the nails are shortened, allowing you to trim them even shorter next time without hitting the quick.

Remember, just like with a brush, introduce the clippers to your dog from early on so he is used to them when it's time to trim his nails. Reward him with a treat when you pull the clippers out, so he establishes a positive association. This will make trimming his nails less stressful for both him and you.

Cleaning the Ears and Eyes

Regular ear and eye cleaning help to prevent infections. To clean your dog's ears, simply squeeze the cleaning solution into one ear as the bottle directs. You may need an extra set of hands to help with this if your Mastiff is unwilling.

*Photo Courtesy
of Sabrina Walston*

Once the solution is in, massage the ear canal for a minute, then move on to the next ear. Don't be alarmed if your Mastiff shakes his head afterward, as this is totally normal.

Wipe his eyes clean with an eye cleaning wipe to remove any dust or pollen. Do this as often as needed or at least once a month. This can also greatly help with allergies.

Brushing Teeth

Take your Mastiff to the vet every year or two for a professional dental cleaning. Dental health is often neglected or overlooked when it comes to dogs, but good oral care can greatly impact a canine's overall health for the better. Dogs can suffer from the same oral diseases and pains that humans do, which can lead to debilitating pain and even difficulty eating if left untreated.

In between professional cleanings, you should be brushing your dog's teeth regularly at home with a dog-specific toothpaste and brush. Due to the overwhelming number of older dogs with periodontal disease, some experts recommend you brush your dog's teeth on the same schedule you brush yours—twice a day. Never use human toothpaste, as it is very different from dog-specific toothpaste and can even contain xylitol, a substance that is toxic to dogs.

There are several types of dog toothbrushes to choose from. There is a standard one-sided brush that looks much like the kind we use, there is a three-sided brush designed to fit around your dog's teeth while you brush, and there are even brushes that fit over your finger and sonic brushes. Choose what your dog prefers and tolerates the best.

Introduce the toothbrush as early as possible. Here is a helpful step-by-step.

1. Choose a calm time to introduce your dog to the toothbrushing process.

2. Begin by gently touching your dog's teeth and gums before introducing the brush.

3. Add dog toothpaste to your finger and allow him to become accustomed to the taste and sensation by gently rubbing his teeth with it.

4. As your dog becomes comfortable, introduce the brush with toothpaste by gently putting it in his mouth and brushing his teeth in a circular motion. Make sure you get all the way to the back, but take it slow and allow your Mastiff to become comfortable with it before pushing it on him to avoid resistance and fear. If your dog becomes fearful, stop the brushing and try again another day.

5. Remember to praise your dog constantly as you are brushing his teeth. This is an unnatural experience for him, and it may take some extra encouragement for him to become comfortable.

6) Reward with a treat after you are finished to provide a positive association.

Brushing is important, but there are other ways of protecting your dog's dental health as well. Chewing has been shown to naturally reduce plaque and tartar build-up. Make sure you get a dental chew large enough for an English Mastiff and supervise him with it so that he doesn't choke.

Photo Courtesy of Jennifer Tapscott

CHAPTER 13
Basic Health Care

Visiting the Vet

Your Mastiff pup will see the vet several times in the first year to receive his vaccinations, but your dog will need to continue to see the vet once a year for routine check-ups after that. These regular vet visits are simply a check-up and are meant to make sure your Mastiff is well and healthy. It's important to take your dog to the vet regularly so that any potential issues or diseases are caught and treated early.

At these appointments, the vet will listen to your dog's heart and lungs, examine the ears, eyes, nose, and mouth, and do an abdominal examination. The vet may also draw blood to check for heartworms and take stool samples to screen for other parasites. He may also want to observe your dog's gait and examine his coat condition.

These appointments are a great time to ask your vet any questions you may have about your Mastiff. Make a list so that you don't forget. Also, be ready to answer questions your vet may have about your Mastiff, such as diet, activity level, or any other routines.

Photo Courtesy
of Jessica Rose
Big Paw Mastiffs

Fleas

Fleas are the most common parasite to affect dogs around the world. Fleas reproduce quickly, meaning one single flea picked up on a daily walk can lead to an infestation that is difficult to control. Luckily, flea prevention is easy and effective, and there are several methods to protect your dog from these parasites.

Topical Flea Medication: Topical flea preventative is a popular option that is readily available and affordable. This medication comes in a small tube that you squeeze onto your Mastiff's back, between the shoulder blades. This medication takes about 12 hours to go into effect and lasts about 30 days, meaning monthly application is required for continued protection. These medications often have a minimum age, so consult your vet before beginning.

Photo Courtesy of Bonnie Brown

Photo Courtesy
of Ashia Cosey

This topical solution absorbs into your dog's bloodstream and circulates through his entire body. When a flea bites anywhere on your dog's body, not just where the medication was applied, it is killed and unable to reproduce and cause infestation. While this method of prevention is effective and cheap, it does leave a greasy spot on your dog's back for several days. Take care not to come into contact with this medication and keep all children away from the area until it is fully absorbed.

Oral Flea Medication: Another common method of flea preventative is an oral medication. These tablets typically prevent both fleas and ticks for 30 days, so monthly doses are required. Some oral tablets even prevent heartworm and internal parasites as well.

While these are easy to administer, they are more expensive than topical treatments, and there are potential side effects, just as with any medication. These side effects include skin irritation, vomiting, and diarrhea. These are typically mild but always seek vet care if your dog has a negative reaction to his medication.

Flea Collars: Flea collars are collars covered in topical flea medication, typically permethrin. These collars are worn in addition to your dog's collar with identification. These collars offer the benefit of up to eight months of protection, but they can also cause skin irritation and even toxicity in cats. Just like with topical applications, avoid contact with the flea collar so that you aren't absorbing the medication into your skin as well.

Flea collars should be used with care and should never be used on a young puppy. Again, consult your vet before beginning any flea treatment or preventative.

Even if your dog lives primarily indoors, he will need to be on a flea preventative. One trip outside to relieve himself is all it takes to pick up one flea and begin an infestation. If your Mastiff happens to ingest a flea, he may become infected with tapeworm, which requires medication to clear. Fleas can also cause an allergic reaction in your dog, causing severe shedding, sores, and even loss of fur.

If the infestation is severe, anemia can occur. Check your Mastiff's gums and the insides of his eyelids for a pale or white color. If you notice a loss of color in these areas, call your vet immediately, as your dog is likely suffering from anemia.

How to Treat an Infestation

Fleas are very difficult to get rid of, but there are a few things you can do. If your dog has fleas, skip the flea bath. The shampoos used only kill the live fleas on your dog and not the eggs and larvae, meaning they are a temporary solution. Not only do these flea shampoos not address the whole problem, but they are full of harmful chemicals that your dog doesn't need to be exposed to. Instead, use Dawn dish soap for the exact same result minus the irritation from the medicated shampoo.

HELPFUL TIP
Feeding Tips

Being a giant breed dog, English Mastiffs are prone to the potentially deadly bloat. To help prevent bloat, feed your Mastiff 2 to 3 times per day instead of one large meal. Don't let them exercise vigorously within half an hour of eating. Also, try to prevent them from gulping their food too quickly. Slow feeder bowls can help prevent gulping.

You will also need to purchase a flea comb and carefully comb through your dog's fur, all the way down to the skin at a 45-degree angle. These combs are designed with closely spaced teeth that fleas cannot pass between. Comb your entire Mastiff, but focus on the head, neck, and tail, as this is where fleas love to hide.

If you find a flea in the comb, trap it in a wet paper towel, then drop it in soapy water to kill it. Act quickly, as the fleas move quickly and can jump from the comb once exposed.

Once you have addressed the fleas on your Mastiff, shift the focus to your home, as there may be fleas lurking there as well, waiting to reinfest your dog. Vacuum every area from the floor to the curtains twice a day to ensure the fleas are picked up as they hatch. Empty the vacuum after each time, and take it outside so any living fleas cannot reenter your home. Do this for two weeks in order to get rid of all the fleas as they hatch. Remember, fleas are rapid reproducers, so don't forget.

Photo Courtesy of Erin Neuman

Ticks

Ticks often go unnoticed by your dog and you, but they pose a much greater health threat to your pooch. Ticks are notorious for spreading serious diseases to both dog and human hosts. While most ticks prefer your Mastiff as a host, he won't hesitate to bite you if given the opportunity.

Lyme Disease: This common tick-borne disease carries a serious risk for both humans and dogs. Transmitted by the black-legged tick, also called the deer tick, this disease is present across the United States, but it is more prevalent in the northeast.

Lyme Disease in dogs presents much as it does in humans, with flu-like symptoms, such as fever, chills, aches, and swollen lymph nodes. These signs can be difficult to detect in dogs, so watch for any change in behavior, apparent discomfort, or loss of appetite. If caught early, Lyme Disease can typically be treated successfully with an antibiotic, but prompt treatment is a must, so do not delay treatment.

If your vet suspects Lyme Disease, he will perform a C6 test to detect antibodies. This disease cannot be passed from an infected dog to a human or another dog. It can only be transmitted via tick bite.

Anaplasmosis: Symptoms of anaplasmosis are similar to Lyme Disease but also include low platelets, which is usually made evident by unusual bleeding or bruising. This disease is typically found in the northeast United States, the upper Midwest, and the western coastal states.

Canine Ehrlichiosis: This tick-borne illness is found all over the world. Symptoms include loss of appetite, low platelets, and fever. If you notice your Mastiff is unwell after a tick bite, take him to the vet promptly to avoid chronic symptoms that are difficult to manage.

Rocky Mountain Spotted Fever: This is another common tick-borne disease that affects both humans and animals. It is typically found in ticks around the United States and in Central and South America. Symptoms of Rocky Mountain Spotted Fever are similar to others and include fever, loss of appetite, joint pain, low platelets, swollen lymph nodes, and occasionally neurological signs.

Babesiosis: Babesiosis can cause hemolysis—a breakdown of red blood cells, causing symptoms like jaundice, pale gums, dark urine, lethargy, depression, and sometimes enlargement of the spleen. This disease can be fatal, so seek care for your Mastiff immediately.

Tick Prevention

Ticks and fleas are often treated using the same medication, as discussed in the previous section. Make sure your dog's preventative covers both fleas and ticks to help your Mastiff avoid serious infection and disease.

Aside from medication, take care to avoid tall grass or brush, as this is where ticks are likely to be. If your Mastiff does go through brush or tall grass, inspect him promptly when you get home and remove any ticks you find with the following steps.

(1) With gloves, use tweezers to grab the tick firmly and as close to the skin as possible.

(2) Once you securely have the tick, pull straight up so that none of the tick's mouth parts are left behind, causing infection.

(3) Put the tick in a jar of soapy water to kill it and clean the tick bite area thoroughly with antiseptic.

(4) Keep the tick for identification purposes in the event your dog begins showing symptoms. These may take up to two weeks to present, so watch your Mastiff closely for changing behavior.

Though both ticks and fleas can be seasonal in many regions, most vets recommend keeping your dog on a year-round preventative.

Worms and Parasites

Worms and parasites are common in dogs, but they can become harmful if left untreated. These common worms and parasites include hookworm, ringworm, roundworms, tapeworms, whipworms, coccidia, giardia, and spirochetes. These parasites are typically diagnosed via a stool sample, but there are some signs and symptoms you can watch for as well.

Hookworm: Hookworm larvae live in the soil and can be picked up through common activities such as walking through a park. These worms attach themselves to the intestinal walls and feed off your dog's blood. Diarrhea and weight loss are possible signs of hookworms.

Once your vet confirms a diagnosis, oral medication can be used to treat the parasite. Depending on the severity of the infestation, iron supplements may be needed to treat anemia. Young puppies are most susceptible to hookworms, as is the case with most parasites.

Ringworm – This is actually a fungus and not a worm. Ringworm causes circular bald patches on your dog's skin and is easily spread from dog to dog and even dog to human, in some cases. Your vet will probably treat your dog with a medicated shampoo and an oral medication.

Roundworm – Roundworms are common and typically discovered when the owner spots round white worms in a dog's stool. These worms are typically an inch or two in length. Other symptoms of roundworm include coughing, vomiting, and diarrhea; however, these only present in severe cases. Ringworms can also be passed to humans, especially kids.

Tapeworm: Tapeworm is commonly caused by ingesting larvae, typically by eating a flea. Weight loss and diarrhea are common symptoms, as well as small worm segments in your dog's stool. These often resemble grains of rice. Treatment includes an oral medication and possible injections.

Whipworms: Whipworms live in the large intestine and are difficult to spot in a stool sample. Signs of infection may include a mucus covering at the tip of your dog's stool. These parasites are typically not serious but can cause weight loss. Treatment includes an oral medication.

Coccidia, Giardia, and Spirochetes: These are not worms but are single-celled parasites that can do much damage to your dog before you even know he is infected. These parasites can cause lasting diseases and issues for a dog and require swift treatment from a vet. Often transmitted through water, food, soil, and feces, these parasites live in unsanitary conditions.

Young puppies and older dogs are more susceptible due to their weakened immune systems. Oral medication is needed.

Heartworm: Heartworms are much more severe than other intestinal parasites. These worms are transmitted via mosquito bite and typically take anywhere from six to seven months to develop into adult heartworms, which live in your dog's heart and cause major issues. These worms can cause lung, heart, and artery damage that may be permanent.

Treatment at the earliest sign of infection is crucial and may be the difference between life or death for your Mastiff. Early symptoms include loss of appetite, cough, fatigue, and no motivation to get moving or play. As the disease progresses, these symptoms will become more severe and include bloating and even heart failure.

Heartworms are common in the southern portion of the United States, especially around the Gulf of Mexico; however, cases have been recorded in all 50 states. Preventative medication should be started around the six-month mark. Options for this preventative include topical, oral, and injection.

Your vet will most likely require yearly heartworm testing for your Mastiff, even if he is on preventative. This disease is very dangerous and difficult to treat. If your dog is diagnosed with heartworm disease, treatment can cost anywhere from $500 to $1,500, and it isn't guaranteed to work.

Vaccinations

Vaccinations are an important aspect of keeping your Mastiff healthy and safe from a potentially life-threatening illness. These vaccines work by injecting the body with antigens to elicit an immune response producing antibodies for those diseases. While your dog does not actually contract the disease after injection, the antibodies are able to form and build immunity to the disease going forward.

Distemper, adenovirus, hepatitis, parvovirus, and parainfluenza are considered the core vaccinations that every puppy should receive when nursing ends at about six weeks of age. These shots are usually given in four rounds: once at six weeks, 10 weeks, 14 weeks, and 18 weeks. Many vets prefer to administer these vaccines in one shot, called a 5-Way. Depending on where you live and your dog's risk factors, your vet may also recommend vaccinations for Bordetella and Leptospirosis.

The rabies vaccine is required legally in most areas and is administered separately, no sooner than 12 weeks of age. This vaccine must be administered every one to three years.

While these vaccines are safe and effective, negative reactions can occur. Allergic reactions to vaccinations can cause hives, swelling, vomiting, and fever. Notify your vet immediately of any negative reactions, even if mild. The symptoms could worsen after the next round of shots.

Oftentimes, but not always, vaccinations are required to access many dog-related facilities. These may include kennels for boarding or daycare, groomers, and sometimes, training facilities. Be sure to keep access to vaccination records in case you need to show proof.

Common Diseases and Conditions in English Mastiffs

> 66
>
> *Mastiffs are prone to several genetic health concerns, including heart, hip, and elbow issues due to their massive size. Keeping your Mastiff at a healthy weight is important, as well as getting a puppy from parents that have been health-tested. This will greatly reduce your chances of health issues.*
>
> **MELISSA COX**
> *Ozark Valley Mastiffs*
> 99

Bloat: Bloat, formally known as gastric dilatation and volvulus, is common in English Mastiffs. This is when your dog's stomach fills with gas and twists, cutting off the blood supply to the stomach, and sometimes, the spleen. Symptoms include dry heaving, restlessness, or an enlarged abdomen. Your Mastiff may also lay with his head on his feet with his backside in the air.

Bloat can happen quickly and potentially turns fatal in as little as half an hour, so early detection is crucial. Take your dog to an animal hospital immediately if you suspect bloat.

Bone and Joint Disease: Mastiffs can suffer from a number of bone and joint issues. Hip and elbow dysplasia are both commonly inherited diseases. This is when the joints develop improperly, which can lead to painful rubbing, arthritis, and even lameness. If you notice your dog moving painfully or getting up slower than usual, have him checked for dysplasia. The sooner it is caught, the more successful treatment is, typically.

X-rays can determine the severity of the dysplasia. In life-hindering situations, surgery may be the best option to give your Mastiff a full and happy life.

Photo Courtesy
of Samantha Davey

Wobbler Syndrome: This is a neurological disease commonly found in Mastiffs. It causes your dog to have a "wobbly" or unsteady gait. This occurs when there is a narrowing of the vertebrae in the neck, which pinches the spinal cord and associated nerves. This can cause neck pain and other nervous system issues, including weakness.

The first symptoms of Wobbler syndrome are often unsteady back legs and stumbling, but can also be severe pain in the neck. Most Mastiffs with Wobbler syndrome will present and be diagnosed before the age of three.

Non-surgical treatment for Wobbler syndrome focuses on pain management and swelling. Activity may be limited, and NSAIDs may be prescribed to decrease swelling of the affected tissues. Medications will probably need to be increased and altered as the disease progresses.

Surgical treatment involves fusing the spine in the affected areas. After this procedure, your Mastiff will remain in the hospital for recovery. Activity will be limited for 2–3 months after. There is a small chance of major complications with this surgery, and approximately 20 percent of dogs will have reoccurring Wobbler syndrome even after. On the other side, about 25 percent of dogs treated with medication can remain stable without surgery.

Discuss options and outcomes with your vet if your dog has Wobbler syndrome.

Kidney Stones: Cystinuria is a genetic metabolic defect of the kidneys. This defect causes the kidneys to not reabsorb cystine properly, which leads to stones and infections. If you see blood in his urine or your dog's urinary patterns change, seek vet care.

Bone Cancer: Osteosarcoma is the most common cause of death for English Mastiffs. This cancer is not detectable by genetic testing, so be sure your breeder doesn't have a history of cancer in their bloodlines.

Symptoms of this cancer are lameness, masses or lumps, and swelling. If you notice any of these changes in your Mastiff, see the vet as soon as possible. Early detection is essential for positive outcomes with osteosarcoma.

Eye Conditions: English Mastiffs are prone to several eye conditions, the most serious of which is progressive retinal atrophy (PRA). This is a degenerative eye disease that progresses slowly into complete blindness, often by middle age.

A DNA test can detect PRA in English Mastiffs, so ask your breeder if your pup's bloodline is free of carriers. Other eye conditions that affect Mastiffs are eyelid deformities, cherry eye, cataracts, and retinal dysplasia.

Heart Disease: There are several heart conditions that commonly affect the English Mastiff. These include cardiomyopathy, pulmonic stenosis, mitral dysplasia, and subaortic stenosis. Your vet should screen for these conditions regularly, and your Mastiff's bloodlines should be free of any heart conditions.

Other Notable Conditions: Epilepsy, hypothyroidism, allergies, and skin problems are also common for the breed. If you notice any behavior changes in your Mastiff, take him to the vet to rule out any diseases and conditions.

Holistic Alternatives and Supplements

Whether you are looking for a way to treat your sick Mastiff, or you're just seeking preventative care, a healthy dog begins with a healthy lifestyle. This includes proper diet and exercise. Holistic alternatives are also becoming more and more common. These alternatives have been used for centuries and are getting some attention back in the spotlight as of late.

ACUPUNCTURE

Acupuncture involves pricking the skin or tissues with needles. It has notable benefits for managing pain and increasing circulation. Supporting overall wellness, acupuncture can aid in the treatment of hip dysplasia, allergies, gastrointestinal problems, and pain due to cancer treatments.

Acupuncture causes no pain and is shown to have a calming effect on pets. Though this is a promising alternative to medications, you should always consult your veterinarian before beginning any treatment. Acupuncture should only be performed by a certified acupuncturist.

HERBS

Not all herbs are safe for your English Mastiff. Some can interact with medications your dog may be taking and have unintentional ill effects. Discuss all herbs with your vet before adding them to your dog's diet or lifestyle. Some commonly used herbs include:

Goldenseal: Anti-inflammatory and anti-bacterial, goldenseal can be used externally on bodily infections or as an eyewash for infections or conjunctivitis. It can be taken internally at the first sign of kennel cough or digestive issues and can also be beneficial in the treatment of tapeworms and giardia. Goldenseal should not be used for too long as it can cause stress on the liver.

Milk Thistle: Milk thistle may protect against liver damage. If your dog is on any medication that can damage his liver, discuss adding milk thistle to his regimen with your vet.

Ginger: Just as with people, ginger is an effective tool for treating nausea and cardiovascular conditions in dogs. Ginger has cardiotonic effects and can promote the functionality of the heart.

Chamomile: Another herb that aids digestion, relieves muscle spasms, and reduces inflammation, chamomile is a great option for treating chronic bowel and gas disorders and can also ease your dog's anxiety.

Licorice: Licorice root is a fast-acting anti-inflammatory that can be used to treat arthritis and other inflammatory diseases. It has been shown to enhance the efficacy of other herbs, so it is often combined with others as a part of a treatment plan.

CBD Oil: The American Kennel Club's website states, "Currently, there has been no formal study on how CBD affects dogs. What scientists do know is that cannabinoids interact with the endocannabinoid receptors located in the central and peripheral nervous systems, which help maintain balance in the body and keep it in a normal healthy state."

CBD oil, also known as cannabidiol, is thought to treat pain and help control seizures in dogs. Anecdotal evidence also shows that CBD oil may have anti-inflammatory, anti-cancer, anti-anxiety, and cardiac benefits. Discuss with your vet the option of adding a CBD supplement to your dog's lifestyle.

This is not a comprehensive list, but only a few of the common herbs used for dogs. If you want your dog to experience the benefits of herbal remedies but can't source the herbs yourself, there are many premade solutions and tinctures available, conveniently packaged and mixed with directions. This can help ensure you are using the herb correctly.

Only use herbs and supplements from reputable and trustworthy companies. Beware of cheaper products that may contain synthetics. And always consult your vet before beginning any herbal treatment for your Mastiff.

Pet Insurance

Pet insurance is an option for Mastiffs; however, this option needs to be carefully researched. While pet insurance can protect you in the event any conditions arise, it can also be costly and unbeneficial. Each company offers different coverage, so be sure to read the fine print and understand any exclusions; there is almost always an annual deductible you must meet before insurance will cover any costs. Even after that is met, many policies only cover 80 percent, with wellness exams and vaccines not included.

Rates will depend on your dog's age and condition. Unless something considerable comes up, it may be more affordable to simply pay out of pocket for services. Ask your vet what pet insurance he recommends, and go from there.

CHAPTER 14
Nutrition

> " Probably the biggest misconception about owning a Mastiff is thinking that they must eat a lot! In all actuality, a Mastiff doesn't eat any more than a German Shepherd because their energy level is so laid back. I often refer to my Mastiffs as moving ottomans, as they are a welcome place to rest my feet.
>
> **TERRY LATVA**
> *North Texas Mastiffs* "

Benefits of a Quality Dog Food

A healthy and balanced diet is just as important for your English Mastiff as it is for you. Proper nutrition is the best way to set your dog up for a healthy life. As humans, we do our best to avoid processed foods and additives, and those same principles apply to your Mastiff.

Dogs require their own balance of protein, fats, carbs, vitamins, and minerals to stay healthy. Choose a dog food that is made with quality ingredients, without preservatives and fillers, to ensure your dog has a chance at optimal health. While all commercial dog foods are required to meet minimum standards, minimum standards are not going to provide your dog with the best nutrition and will not promote a healthy lifestyle.

According to Dr. Hugh Stevenson, a veterinarian in Ontario, Canada, symptoms of poor nutrition include a dull, thin coat, cracking or bleeding footpads, weight problems, excess stool and gas, and passing undigested grain particles in feces. Quality nutrition leads to a lustrous coat, healthy skin and weight, and less stool due to more of the food being digestible.

This next section will walk you through the basics of dog foods to help you understand and determine what is best for your Mastiff.

66

I feed a raw diet and believe all dogs deserve to be. If you choose to feed kibble, puppies must be kept as close to a 1:1 phosphorus/calcium ratio as possible and a low (under 26%) protein level to prevent rapid growth, which can damage the growth plates. Generally, puppy foods are not good choices, and most Mastiff breeders skip puppy food and wean puppies straight to adult food to match their nutritional needs.

AMANDA GRIFFIN
Gryphon Mastiffs

99

Types of Commercial Dog Foods

Dog foods come in several varieties, including dry, wet, fresh, and even a combination of dry and wet. You may be overwhelmed at the number of options for your Mastiff, but understanding the basics of each type of food can help you choose what is best for your dog.

Wet Dog Food: If you have ever been near wet dog food, you know it has an undeniably strong smell. This may be a drawback for you, but this is actually a great way to get a picky dog to eat his food. Wet food also helps with hydration for a dog that doesn't drink as much water as he should.

Photo Courtesy of Nicole Meeker

Wet dog food does have a few cons, however. It spoils quickly after opening, so it cannot be left out for a dog to graze on all day. If it's not eaten promptly, it will need to be refrigerated. Canned food is also a bit pricier than its common dry counterpart, especially for a giant breed such as the Mastiff.

Dry Dog Food: Dry dog food is shelf-stable after opening, has minimal smell, and can even help to clean your dog's teeth while he chews. Not all dry kibbles are created equally, so if you choose to go this route, make sure you choose one with the highest-quality ingredients, which we will discuss later in this chapter.

Dehydrated Dog Food: Dehydrated dog food typically begins the process raw, so it is nutritionally similar to a raw diet. Proponents of this type of dog food claim that it has all the benefits of a nutrition-packed raw diet, with none of the risks.

Dehydrated dog food can be safely kept for up to 12 months without the use of preservatives. Because it isn't cooked prior, it retains more nutrients than other dry options. Freeze-drying is another way to produce dehydrated dog food with the same benefits.

Raw Food Diet: There are now several companies that sell raw food options in the refrigerated pet food section that carry less risk than a home-made raw diet. Discuss the pros and cons of a raw food diet with your vet because it is controversial. While some believe it has incredible health benefits, others claim that long term, a raw food diet can lead to issues caused by an unbalanced diet.

> *Because of their rapid growth rate, a food low in protein and with an equal ratio of calcium to phosphorous is very important. Keeping your dog lean will help with joint issues down the road.*
>
> **LISA ARMSTRONG**
> *Epic Mastiffs*

Ingredients to Avoid

Reading a dog food label can be difficult and confusing. Sometimes it may even seem like it's written in a different language! Companies that produce low-quality foods often include vague terms and scientific words to persuade the customer that they actually have a quality food, even when that may not be the case. Below is a list of ingredients to watch for and avoid when choosing a commercial food to feed your Mastiff.

BHA/BHT: Studies are not conclusive, but these chemical preservatives have been linked to hyperactivity and cancer. Used to preserve fats in human food and pet food, BHA and BHT have been banned in some countries but

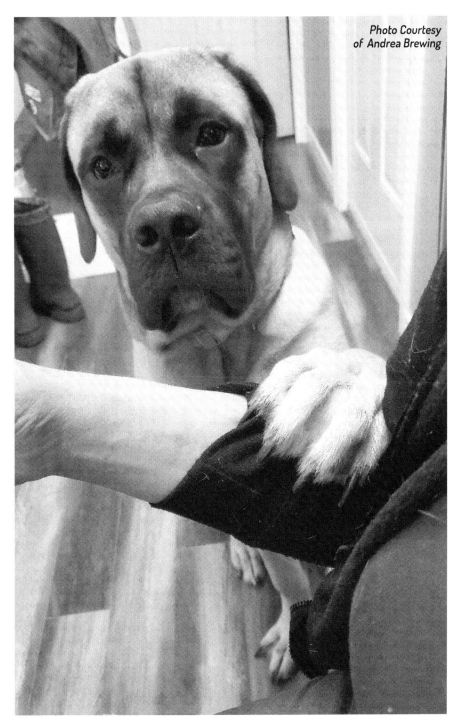

*Photo Courtesy
of Andrea Brewing*

are still allowed in the United States, Canada, and Europe. It's best to avoid these potentially harmful ingredients.

Meat, Meat Meal, or Rendered Fat: Any time you see a vague, nonspecific term such as "meat" or "meat meal," you can bet these are the lowest-quality ingredients allowed. These are often leftover things from slaughterhouses that get included in your dog's food. These terms can even include leftover, expired meat from the grocery store or diseased livestock.

Instead, look for specific meat terms, such as chicken, salmon, turkey, lamb, and beef. If your dog food contains salmon or salmon meal, make sure it's labeled "wild-caught." Farm-raised salmon is less nutrient-dense than its wild counterpart because of the unnatural diet the fish are fed and has been found to potentially contain more contaminants.

Nitrites and Nitrates: These are chemical additives used to preserve freshness and extend the shelf life of meat products. Nitrates and nitrites are found in human and dog food and should be avoided at all costs. Sodium nitrite can be toxic to your dog in high doses and has been linked to cancer.

Soy: Soy is cheap and readily available, so dog food manufacturers use it as an inexpensive way to boost the protein percentage of the food. However, it can be difficult for your dog to digest and can cause gastrointestinal upset.

Other ingredients to watch out for include meat by-products, sodium hexametaphosphate, food dyes, carrageenan, taurine, cellulose, artificial flavors, and corn syrup. Dog food manufacturers dedicated to producing a quality, superior dog food will not use these red-flag ingredients. Though high-quality dog foods can be a bit more expensive, the cost is worth it, and it may even save you money in vet bills in the long term by providing your Mastiff with the best nutrition and the healthiest life possible.

> **"**
>
> *One feeding tip I have is to feed your dog outside if possible to avoid the big head shake of slobber after eating or drinking. Be sure to have a cloth ready to wipe his mouth or anything else that gets drooled on.*
>
> **CAROL SIMS**
> *Sims English Mastiffs*
>
> **"**

Photo Courtesy of Sabrina Walston

Grain-Free Diet

There has been a recent trend in grain-free dog food. Proponents believe that because wolves in the wild don't consume more than a trace number of grains, domesticated dogs shouldn't either. However, dogs are not genetically identical to wolves, and they have adapted to effectively utilize grains in their diet.

Grain-free dog food contains other plants instead of grains. These include peas, lentils, potatoes, and legumes. These plant sources provide the starch to make the kibble and an added protein boost, allowing the manufacturer to cut back on more expensive animal proteins. This can lead to a depletion of the amino acid taurine.

Taurine is found in animal proteins but not in plant proteins, and the FDA has linked this to a rise of cardiomyopathy in dogs who have been fed a grain-free diet. It is best to discuss with your vet what food is best for your dog before following any food trends, as they could have serious implications on your dog's health in the short term and long term.

Photo Courtesy
of Jeanie Vega

Homemade Dog Food

The only true way to know exactly what your Mastiff is eating is to make his food yourself. Dogs should have a high-protein diet with limited wheat, corn, and soy. For optimal health, invest the time and resources to make a nutrition-packed meal at home.

Homemade dog food can provide the freshest and best nutrition for your dog. It can be a great source of wholesome, balanced whole-food nutrition without the preservatives commonly found in commercial types. Commercial food is also processed at a high temperature, causing a loss of nutrients that doesn't occur with fresh, homemade food.

While it may seem like a no-brainer to feed your dog a homemade diet, it's crucial that you discuss a recipe with your vet before attempting this diet. A homemade diet needs to be carefully planned and should contain the right balance of nutrients for your Mastiff, or it could lead to a host of health issues down the road.

Table Food 101

It may be tempting to feed your Mastiff table food, especially when those adorable eyes are staring up at you, silently pleading for a bite. It's important to know what is safe to share and what is not. In Chapter 3, we discussed a list of foods to never feed your dog, so you may want to return there and refresh your memory before continuing on to this list of foods that are okay to share with your pup.

If you wish to share foods with your Mastiff, there are several things you can share safely. Just remember that these foods should be shared in moderation as a treat or snack. If your dog isn't eating his regular food at mealtime, cut back on the snacks so you don't throw off his nutritional balance.

- White and brown rice
- Cooked eggs
- Oatmeal
- Carrots
- Cheese (It is possible for some dogs to be lactose intolerant.)
- Peanut butter (without xylitol)
- Berries
- Green beans
- Seedless watermelon
- Bananas
- Peas
- Pineapple
- Apples
- Broccoli
- Potatoes

These foods should be somewhat plain, avoiding any heavy seasonings that may upset your dog's stomach. This is not a comprehensive list, and different sensitivities can exist from dog to dog, so consult your vet if your Mastiff appears to have a food allergy or sensitivity.

Photo Courtesy
of Dylan Rook

Weight Management

Weight management is crucial for dogs to maintain a healthy and well lifestyle. An overweight Mastiff can become more susceptible to diseases and illnesses. If your Mastiff is or becomes overweight, discuss options to bring his weight down with your vet immediately.

One of the best ways to help your Mastiff maintain a healthy weight is by helping him get adequate exercise. Refer back to chapter 9 for fun ways to keep your dog active.

HELPFUL TIP
Watch Protein Levels

Protein is the building block of muscles, so that means it's important in large breed dogs like Mastiffs, right? Actually, you want to make sure the food you give your English Mastiff isn't too high in protein, especially when they are a puppy. That's because a diet high in protein can make your puppy grow too quickly and develop bone or joint problems. Look for puppy food designed for large breed dogs. It should contain less than 30% protein.

It may be beneficial to reevaluate your dog's diet and food as well. Is he getting a quality food, or is he eating a food with extra fillers, causing your dog to eat more to compensate for fewer nutrients? Switching to a higher-quality dog food is a great place to start if your dog's weight becomes an issue.

If you're making homemade food for your Mastiff, and he is having weight management issues, seek the advice of a vet or pet nutritionist. You may need to alter the recipe or portion sizes to better fit your dog's needs.

If you have tried all of the above and your Mastiff is still overweight, discuss options with your vet. He may suggest a weight-management food that has higher protein, lower fat, and fewer calories. Never give weight-management foods to a puppy, as these are formulated specifically with adult dogs in mind.

CHAPTER 15
Dealing with Unwanted Behaviors

What Is Considered Bad Behavior?

Just like humans, dog personalities vary, with some being calmer and others spunkier. Just because a dog is exhibiting a behavior that you may find annoying doesn't make it "bad." So, when it comes to bad behavior in dogs, how can we know what is actually considered "bad" and in need of correction? Below is a list of common behaviors in dogs that are often considered bad but may not be.

Photo Courtesy of Hayley Stangl

Barking: While excessive barking may be a nuisance, barking is a natural form of communication for your Mastiff and shouldn't be punished. Mastiffs are not known for barking a lot; however, it may become an issue in certain circumstances, and you may need to correct the annoyance.

Is there a consistent trigger, such as seeing other dogs or people, that is causing your dog to bark? If so, focus on socializing your dog so that he becomes more comfortable at the sight of others. If his triggers are more inconsistent and unpredictable, determine if your Mastiff may be trying to tell you something. Does he have enough stimulation? Is he getting enough attention?

If you are having an issue with excessive barking, fill a soda bottle halfway with rocks or coins and shake it every time he barks. Tell him "quiet" in a calm voice and reward him with a small treat when he stops. Continue this method until he learns to be "quiet" on command.

HELPFUL TIP
Separation Anxiety

English Mastiffs are the ultimate companion dog, and they hate to be left home alone. As a result, they are prone to separation anxiety that may cause destructive behavior. If you work long hours, you may want to consider taking your Mastiff to doggie daycare, so they aren't home alone as much.

If barking while you are away is a problem, see the section on Separation Anxiety in chapter 5 for ways to keep your Mastiff calm while you are gone. While some owners resort to vocal cord operations such as devocalization or shock collars to keep their dogs quiet, these are cruel punishments for a canine behavior that isn't inherently bad.

Chasing: The English Mastiff, in general, does not have a particularly strong prey drive, but chasing can still be a problem for a spunky, energetic Mastiff. While this behavior can be annoying and dangerous, it should never be treated as "bad" behavior. Your dog is only doing what comes naturally to him. Obedience training can help the issue but may not ever stop it completely.

Though not a bad behavior, chasing can be dangerous, especially in a city with lots of cars and other hidden dangers. Unless you can be sure he won't chase a neighborhood cat or a skateboarder riding down the street, you will need to keep your Mastiff leashed or contained in a fence the entire time he is out.

Digging: Your Mastiff may have picked up a fondness for digging that you find downright annoying. Even so, this isn't inherently bad behavior and shouldn't be punished. Refer to chapter 5 for more information on how to deal with a digging Mastiff.

Leash Pulling: This can be a major problem for a dog as big a Mastiff, but it is typically the direct result of a lack of training rather than a disobedient dog. Taking the time to teach your dog how to properly walk on a leash can do wonders to eliminate leash tugging. If your Mastiff is pulling the leash when out for a walk, address the problem immediately, as this can quickly become a dangerous situation for the walker.

Other unwanted behaviors that aren't "bad" include chewing up toys and shoes, begging for food, stealing food, jumping up, getting on furniture, and

*Photo Courtesy
of Rose Nelson*

even eating poop. These behaviors are a nuisance but are not evidence of a poorly behaved Mastiff. Rather, they are evidence of a poorly trained Mastiff.

Aggression: Any form of unprovoked aggression should always be considered bad and needs to be dealt with immediately. This may include vicious barking, growling, snarling, or even lunging. If left unchecked, these aggressive behaviors can lead to serious injury or even death for you or your Mastiff. Consult a professional trainer or animal psychologist as soon as you become aware of the aggression. There may be a root issue or trigger that you're unaware of, so do not attempt to fix the issue yourself.

Photo Courtesy of Kara Kamotzki

Finding the Root of the Problem

The first step to eliminating unwanted behavior is to find out why your Mastiff is doing it. Learning why he's exhibiting a certain behavior can make correcting or redirecting the problem much easier for you and your dog.

Instinctual: Many times, unwanted behavior stems from a natural instinct. If this is the case, the behavior will be more challenging to stop. Consult a professional trainer for help, but also try to redirect the instinctual behavior in a positive way. For example, if your Mastiff loves to chase, find a way to let him chase in a controlled environment so he can be safe.

Lack of Training: Most of the unwanted behaviors on this list actually begin with a lack of proper training. Time spent consistently training your dog is the best way to correct these annoyances. See chapter 10 for more training tips and how to get started.

Past Trauma: If you are dealing with aggression issues, consider any traumas in your dog's past, especially if you adopted him later in his life. These issues need to be dealt with by a trained professional, so seek help immediately.

*Photo Courtesy
of Sara Moody*

How to Properly Correct Your English Mastiff

Punishment is not an effective way to correct unwanted behaviors in your Mastiff. Typically, your Mastiff will want to please you with his actions, so if he's doing something undesirable, it's because he isn't sure what is right. Correct him by showing him what you want him to do and not what you don't want him to do. Reward him for positive behavior, and he is sure to catch on quickly.

When to Call a Professional

As mentioned above, these unwanted behaviors are mostly just annoyances. However, sometimes, if left unchecked, they can get out of hand and become a danger to your Mastiff. Digging holes in the yard is irritating, but it becomes a safety issue if he begins digging those holes under the fence. Chewing can be upsetting when your favorite pair of sandals falls victim, but it is not inherently dangerous. On the other hand, chewing on an electrical cord can be deadly.

If your attempts to redirect the behavior have been unsuccessful, seek a professional trainer's help. They have seen these issues time and time again and will have the resources and experience to find a solution that works for both you and your dog. The longer you wait, the harder these bad habits will be to break.

CHAPTER 16

Caring for Your Senior English Mastiff

As your Mastiff begins to age and enters the senior years, he will typically require more medical care and specialized treatment. When they reach their senior years, dogs become more prone to ailments such as arthritis, cognitive dysfunction, cataracts, hearing loss, incontinence, and the inability to regulate body temperature.

While most Mastiffs begin a senior decline between years six to eight, not all Mastiffs will reach this age at the same time, and many dogs can still live happy and healthy lives, even as they age. This chapter will detail potential issues you and your Mastiff may face as he ages and help you navigate the difficult end-of-life decisions when the time comes.

Common Old-Age Ailments

Hearing Loss: A loss of hearing is common for aging dogs. Many Mastiffs lose a degree of hearing but won't go completely deaf. If your dog is suddenly less obedient, is barking more, or is getting startled often, make an appointment with a vet to check his hearing.

If your Mastiff is experiencing hearing loss, you may need to relearn how to communicate with him. Begin this new communication at the first sign of hearing loss so that he has it mastered if his hearing loss progresses. Teach your Mastiff hand signals to accompany any verbal commands you typically give him. It may also be useful to have a flashlight handy to get his attention.

Arthritis: Osteoarthritis is a degenerative joint disease where the cartilage between bones in a joint deteriorates, causing the bones to rub together painfully. This can cause severe pain, stiffness, and even limited mobility. Arthritis cannot be cured but can be managed well with medications and supplements.

Cataracts: Cataracts create an opacity in the lens of the eye, causing blurred vision. These can be progressive, so if you notice a cloudy spot on your dog's eyes, have the vet monitor them carefully for worsening. If left untreated, cataracts can sometimes cause blindness.

Cognitive Dysfunction: Just like humans, senior dogs are susceptible to dementia in their old age. If you notice a behavior change in your older dog, such as forgetfulness or divergence from his normal routine, discuss options with your vet.

If your Mastiff is suffering from cognitive dysfunction, focus on making life easier for him to help ease his confusion and frustration. This may mean putting his food and water in a more visible place so that he doesn't forget where it is or using puppy pads to avoid accidents.

Mental stimulation is crucial for keeping your older dog's mind sharp and functioning properly. Regularly practice routine, basic commands, and play mentally stimulating

HELPFUL TIP
Hip Dysplasia, Arthritis, and Other Joint Problems

Sadly, English Mastiffs are prone to a lot of joint problems. As they age, they may have more trouble walking and getting around on their own. Thick beds can help prevent pressure points on achy joints. You should also have a plan on how to move your Mastiff if they can't get up and you need to take them to the vet.

games such as hide-and-seek. If your dog has dementia, these activities can slow the worsening of symptoms and even help improve memory.

Incontinence: As your Mastiff ages, his ability to hold his bladder diminishes. Take him out more frequently, and keep puppy pads on hand in the house just in case he can't make it out. This is a normal digression and isn't something that should be punished.

Photo Courtesy of Jesse and Jessica Otley

Basic Senior Dog Care

Senior care for your English Mastiff should focus on keeping your dog happy, healthy, and pain-free. Temperature regulation can be more challenging for a senior Mastiff, so be sure to keep your dog out of extreme weather, either hot or cold. Use a sweater to provide him with extra warmth on a cold day, and make sure he has a way to cool off when the weather is hot.

If your Mastiff begins to show symptoms of age, special accommodations can go a long way to make his life easier. For example, a Mastiff with arthritis may have a difficult time with stairs, so keep all of his things on the bottom floor of the house instead. You may even need to invest in a small set of stairs to help him get on the couch more easily or get him a special orthopedic bed to keep him comfortable at night.

Energy levels decline as a dog ages, so adjust your activity expectations to fit what he is now capable of. Gentle exercise, such as slow walking or swimming, is great for an aging dog. Many dogs become obese in their old age due to a lack of activity. This can lead to a worsening of health and old-age ailments such as arthritis. If weight becomes an issue, seek advice from a vet.

Your senior dog will probably need to see the vet more in his last years. The AAHA (American Animal Hospital Association) recommends that you take your senior dog to the vet at least once every six months for a check-up. These regular vet visits can help you catch any conditions early and allow for more prompt treatment, potentially leading to a better quality of life for your Mastiff.

HELPFUL TIP
Lifespan and Common Health Issues

Like most other giant dog breeds, the English Mastiff has a relatively short lifespan of only 6-10 years. This is due in part to the common health issues they face, including:

- **Hip dysplasia** – a painful joint problem where the hip doesn't form properly
- **Gastric torsion (bloat)** – a potentially deadly condition where the stomach fills with air and twists on its axis
- **Osteosarcoma** – an aggressive form of bone cancer that often leads to leg amputation
- **Dilated cardiomyopathy** – a potentially deadly heart condition
- **Progressive retinal atrophy (PRA)** – a degenerative eye condition that usually leads to blindness
- **Hypothyroidism** – a condition where the thyroid gland doesn't produce enough of the thyroid hormone
- **Allergies** – English Mastiffs face both environmental and food allergies
- **Entropion** – a condition where the eyelid rolls inward, causing eyelashes to rub against the eye

Illness and Injury Prevention

Injury and illness are much more challenging to overcome for a senior dog. Care should focus heavily on injury and illness prevention. Though exercise is just as important for your senior Mastiff, it needs to adapt to fit his needs.

Because your aging dog is more prone to injury, exercise should be done slower and with little to no impact on joints. This means no jumping, climbing, or walking at an incline for a prolonged period. Instead, try a slow, leisurely walk or a swim. If you notice your dog limping after exercise, dial it back and take it easier to avoid injury or pain.

Make sure you stay up to date with your Mastiff's vaccinations and medications, including flea and tick preventative. If your elderly dog does become ill, he is more likely to suffer life-threatening complications than his younger counterparts. A case of kennel cough may be no big deal for a young dog, but it could quickly lead to a dangerous case of pneumonia for a senior dog.

Supplements and Nutrition

Good nutrition is still key to keeping your senior dog in his best shape and condition, even in the later years. Quality of life and severity of conditions is directly affected by nutrition, including supplements. Though there are several supplements on the market formulated for senior dogs, always ask your vet before adding anything to your dog's diet, as there is a potential for side effects and drug interactions.

Here is a list of the most common supplements used for senior dogs.

Glucosamine and Chondroitin: Two supplements often paired together to combat osteoarthritis, glucosamine and chondroitin have been found to be therapeutic in the treatment of canine arthritis. These compounds are found naturally in cartilage and are made by the body.

Photo Courtesy of Andrew Ackerman

When looking for a glucosamine and chondroitin supplement, look for highly reputable brands that source all of their ingredients from the United States. Imported glucosamine has been found to contain many contaminants, including lead, especially when sourced from China. Since the FDA does not regulate supplements, the only way to know if you are getting a quality product is to be vigilant and diligent in your research. Even popular pet store brands that say "made in the USA" can include ingredients sourced from China.

Omega-3 Fatty Acids: Omega-3 fatty acids like DHA and EPA have been shown to be beneficial for a number of reasons that may benefit your senior dog. These fatty acids are beneficial for the brain, potentially improving cognitive function in old age, and may even give his immune system a boost. According to the American Kennel Club, "The addition of omega-3 to the diet may [also] help reduce inflammation and can promote cell membrane health."

Antioxidants: Including an extra source of antioxidants in your senior Mastiff's diet can be beneficial as well. You can do this by purchasing a supplement or by simply allowing your dog to snack on high antioxidant fruits, such as berries and apples.

Probiotics: Probiotics help maintain healthy bacteria in the gut, the place where up to 80 percent of a dog's immune defenses reside. This can improve immune function and help your senior dog ward off illness and disease more efficiently.

When it's Time to Say Goodbye

Understanding when it's time to say goodbye and how to do it is one of the hardest aspects of pet ownership. It's a decision no one wants to make, but it is our ultimate responsibility as loving and gracious dog owners. When the time comes, and your Mastiff is experiencing more pain than happiness, it may be time to consider humanely ending his life to relieve him from the pain of his final days.

This is never an easy decision and often leads to an array of emotions for the owner, including sorrow, guilt, and second thoughts. These are normal and will probably never change, no matter how many times you face this decision.

HOW WILL YOU KNOW WHEN THE TIME IS RIGHT?

You and your English Mastiff have formed a bond over your years together that only you can know the depth of. This is why you are the best and only one who should make the final call. If you have a gut feeling that your Mastiff has made a sharp decline in health and is hurting more than not, the time may be right to make the call. A few telltale signs that death is imminent are extreme lethargy, lack of interest in anything, loss of coordination, incontinence, and not eating or drinking.

Only you and your dog will know when this time is. Your dog has trusted you with his life thus far, and he trusts you with it now. If you believe putting him down humanely will end his suffering, speak to your vet and discuss euthanasia.

Once you have made the decision that the time has come to humanely end your dog's suffering, know that second thoughts are normal. This decision will always be hard. Don't second guess the decision that is best for your dog just because it's hard for you. Grieving over this decision, even before it has happened, is natural and normal. Talk to a trusted therapist, friend, or family member to help you cope during this difficult time.

Once you have made the decision, as long as the vet agrees death is inevitable, the process happens fairly quickly. The point is to end your dog's suffering, so there is no sense in putting it off for a few days.

THE EUTHANASIA PROCESS

Before you take your dog to the vet, call anyone who may want to say goodbye to him. Some even choose to host a special day with their dog, feeding him all his favorite foods and taking him to see his favorite spots one last time. If you choose to do this, make it a happy and relaxed day for your dog.

When it's time, you will have the option to be present when the vet performs the procedure. Although it may be hard for you to watch your dog die, know that it will bring your dog comfort and peace in his last moments if you are there with him, holding him, and comforting him.

During the procedure, your vet will administer a solution, typically phenobarbital, intravenously. The solution is usually thick with a blue, pink, or purple tint. The vet may inject it directly into a vein or into an intravenous catheter. Once the solution is injected, it will quickly travel through your dog's body, causing him to lose consciousness within just a few seconds. Your Mastiff will feel no pain. Breathing will slow and then stop altogether. Cardiac arrest will occur and cause death within 30 seconds of the injection.

Your vet will check for signs of life and will most likely step out of the room for a few moments to give you time to say a final goodbye. Your vet and his office staff have been through this before and will understand the emotional weight of the situation for you. They should provide you with privacy and be a source of comfort if needed. Be sure to make payments and after-death arrangements beforehand so you don't have to deal with it after, while you are grieving.

Your dog's body may still move after death, so don't be alarmed if you see twitching. He may also release bodily fluids, and this is also normal. When you are ready, leave your dog and allow the vet to proceed with his remains.

Final Arrangements

Cremation is a common choice for pet owners facing the death of a beloved dog. It is more affordable than a cemetery plot and allows you to keep your dog close to you via his ashes if you choose to do so. If you have chosen to have your dog cremated, your vet will coordinate with a cremation service and notify you when his ashes are ready.

Photo Courtesy of Amanda Koperna

If you are taking your deceased dog home for burial, the vet will place your dog's remains in a container and will typically carry it out to the car for you. Depending on where you live, burying your dog at home may or may not be legal. Check local laws ahead of time.

Even if it is legal, burying your dog at home may not be the best idea. Wild animals may attempt to dig up your Mastiff's remains, floodwaters can cause him to resurface, and even groundwater contamination is possible. If you want to have a memorial at your home, consider spreading his ashes there instead of a burial.

A pet cemetery is another option for a final resting place for your beloved Mastiff. This is a graveyard designated just for pets. The service is not cheap, however. A plot can cost around $400 to $600, and that doesn't include the cost of the casket. While it is pricey, it is a beautiful place for your Mastiff to remain among other beloved pets gone before.

Whichever you choose, once you leave the vet's office, you will begin the grieving process. Grieving the loss of a pet is serious, and you should seek professional help if you are struggling. Just remember, the love and bond that you and your Mastiff shared is not lost with his life on this earth. It remains in your heart and memories forever.

Made in the USA
Middletown, DE
22 December 2024

68065130R00082